Companioning
the Dying

Companioning the Dying

A Soulful Guide for Caregivers

Greg Yoder

Foreword by Alan D. Wolfelt

Companion Press is an imprint of the Center for Loss and Life Transition, 3735 Broken Bow Road, Fort Collins, Colorado 80526, (970) 226-6050, www.centerfor-loss.com.

Companion Press books may be purchased in bulk for sales promotions, premiums and fundraisers. Please contact the publisher at the above address for more information.

Printed in the United States of America.

15 14 13 12 11   5 4 3 2 1

ISBN 978-1-617221-49-1

To the memory of my father, R.K. Yoder,
who taught me to smell the roses.
February 25, 1920-March 29, 1998

And to the memory of Stephanie Vogt
(Sneaky-Snake)—a precious child whose
life and death awakened in me some-
thing that is in no small part responsible
for what I do today. I'll never forget you.
May 26, 1973-August 18, 1987

*Some names have been changed to protect
the privacy of real patients and family
members.*

*Companion Press is dedicated to the education and support of both the
bereaved and bereavement caregivers. We believe that those who companion the bereaved by walking with them as they journey in grief have a
wondrous opportunity: to help others embrace and grow through grief—
and to lead fuller, more deeply-lived lives themselves because of this important ministry.*

For a complete catalog and ordering information,
write or call or visit our website:

Companion
P R E S S

Companion Press
The Center for Loss and Life Transition
3735 Broken Bow Road
Fort Collins, CO 80526
(970) 226-6050
FAX 1-800-922-6051
DrWolfelt@centerforloss.com
www.centerforloss.com

Contents

Part 5 Companioning Children

Preface to the Softcover Edition

When *Companioning The Dying* was published in 2005, my sincere hope was to create a useful and soulful guide to assist those who provide care for the dying. It was in response to more traditional medical model or treatment model ways of thinking, which is our standard in healthcare still today.

I created a comparative table (on page 69) to help the reader understand, at a glance, the difference between Companioning Theory and Treatment Model Theory. I'm reminded the word *treat* comes from the Latin *tractare*, which translates: to drag or pull. While I am grateful for our aggressive treatment model of healthcare for the non-dying population, it's just not a mindset that works in caring for the dying.

The word *companion* consists of *com*, meaning with, and *pan*, which means bread. So to companion another literally means "to share bread with." And relative to the dying, companioning in effect means: *sharing something mutually sustaining with another...something emotionally or spiritually nutritious.* Companioning theory holds that in every shared moment with another, there is simultaneously something being given and received. Always!

Diagnostics and certain treatments are indeed a part of caring for the dying, but Companioning Theory celebrates the one who is dying as the "expert" in his or her experience. It has far more to do with being in relationship than what is said or done. And while those providing the care may be brilliant, skilled and compassionate clinicians, companioning relies on humility and gratitude to guide the use of our virtues without a sense of urgency that something needs to happen. It includes a practice of N.A.T.O. (Not Attached To Outcome). Said another way, companioning the dying means making peace in advance with *any and all* outcomes. It liberates us from the temptation to influence the end-of-life experience of another based on personal bias or some textbook definition of "good death."

The Tenets of Companioning were first written by Dr. Alan Wolfelt, who writes and teaches extensively on companioning the bereaved. Dr. Wolfelt?s highly respected work has touched almost everyone in this country who works with populations who grieve and mourn. With his encouragement, the core of this book was centered around his tenets of companioning the bereaved as they also apply beautifully to companioning the dying.

The response to *Companioning The Dying* has been remarkable for a small printing by today?s standards. The fact that it is going into a second printing is testament to that. I offer a special thanks to the steadfast support of Dr. Wolfelt, Companion Press, and the Center for Loss Bookstore in Fort Collins, Colorado, in making this book accessible to you, the reader. The regular feedback I receive is most gratifying.

In response to the book and seminar I offer, a social worker-bereavement coordinator in hospice wrote to me: "*Several years ago I attended your class at the Center for Loss. Your Companioning the Dying philosophy changed my way of approaching all of my social work practice!*"

Companioning The Dying has been included on the reading list for The Psychology of Death And Dying courses at both the local community college and the major university in my hometown of Tucson, Arizona. Over the years I have received many comments from students expressing appreciation for the ease of reading and usability of the book. One young student shared with me, "*You know, Mr. Yoder, I sell back many of my books after my classes, but yours is one I?ll never get rid of. I?m sure it will continue to help me in my personal and professional life.*"

My sincere hope is that the second printing in paperback will continue to be well-received and utilized as a useful and supportive tool for those who companion the dying. Companioning theory continues to enrich my life and my own daily work with the dying. It keeps me inspired and clear in my role as a hospice counselor in ways I never could have imagined. And to you, dear reader, I wish many blessings to you in your companioning.

Greg Yoder
July 2011

Foreword

Reading *Companioning The Dying* is like sitting around a campfire with a good and trusted friend. There you are in a circle, bundled up to stay warm, savoring a soul-based conversation. Greg Yoder's practical and insightful words, written with candor and a delightful sense of humor, will resonate in your heart and soul. Most important, he reminds us all of what a gift it is to companion another human being who is making the transition from living to dying.

The language we use to describe caring for a dying person exposes our attitudes and beliefs about counseling as well as determines our practices. Because numerous historical roots are deeply embedded in a medical model of psychotherapy, because the medical model appears more scientific than other alternatives, and because the economics of practice are interfaced in a healthcare delivery system, the natural tendency has been to adapt medical model language. Thankfully, this resource doesn't do that!

This resource is anchored in a philosophy of "companioning," not "treating," the dying. I am humbled and honored that Greg has built the contents of this book around my tenets of companioning. Companioning the dying is not about assessing, analyzing, or creating a "good death." Instead, the companioning model is grounded in a "teach me" perspective. It is about learning from and being totally present to another person. I urge you to let Greg help you walk with and learn from those who are willing to be your teachers about death)—and life.

Greg has a genuine and deep commitment to bring care and comfort to the dying. He possesses that rare quality of "congruence"—he is someone who walks his talk, and honors the sacred real-life stories of those around him. It's that quality of authenticity that makes him the right person to pen a book about companioning the dying.

If your passion in life relates to the care of the dying, you will want to read and re-read this book. As a compassionate mentor to others who desire to be present to the dying, Greg will show you how being present to others starts with being present to yourself. He will take you on a journey through the companioning tenets and artfully help you make deep and profound connections with those you are privileged to walk with and learn from.

Fortunately, this book is different than most books you will read related to caring for the dying. It is a refreshing and inspiring departure from more traditional counseling practices. It recognizes that supporting people who are making the transition is more art than science. What I appreciate most about Greg's book is his understanding that spirituality, death, and life are inseparable. A dying soul knows what it needs, and a profound aspect of companioning the dying is to "bear witness" and "give attention" to the deep desires of our fellow human beings. If this resonates with you...read on. Give yourself the gift of this book. As you honor your need to grow in your efforts to provide care to the dying, you will discover how the companioning philosophy presents you with an opportunity to enrich your life and the lives of those you touch.

Enjoy!

Alan Wolfelt

Acknowledgments

For love and support in the writing of this book, I must thank my beloved family: Pamela, love of my life (who thought she would peek at the finished manuscript and find 200 pages filled with "all work and no play make Jack a dull boy;" and my precious children, Rylie, Erin and Thor, and Hannah. You are the bright shining stars of my life.

Thank you Mom-Margaret, Ruth Ann and Gene for your unwavering love and support. Thanks also to Richard, Cyndi, John and Gabe. Cyndi, thank you for your wisdom, honesty and suggestions that gave more clarity to these pages.

To my closest friend, Peter Woods: your friendship is immeasurable. Thanks for tirelessly reading and offering your insight into *Companioning The Dying*.

To Karla Oceanak, thank you for your editing wizardry, and to Angela Hollingsworth for creating the beautiful, artistic structure of this book.

To all my coworkers, friends, colleagues, and fellow companions around the country, I'm grateful to be counted among you as one who is called to work with the dying and bereaved. And to all those patients and families—my teachers—who have and continue to allow me to companion you through your transition from life to death, thank you.

Thanks to Companion Press and the wonderful staff of the Center for Loss and Life Transition, my friends Kathy, Kerri and Pat.

And finally, to my friend and mentor Alan Wolfelt, who first introduced me to "companioning." I offer a sincere thanks for encouragement and guidance on the long road to the completion of this book. Your generous support made *Companioning The Dying* possible.

Introduction

Companioning The Dying is a book meant to help you bring a respectful, nonjudgmental presence to a dying person while liberating you from self-imposed or popular expectations to say or do the right thing. When you companion the dying, how you are inside yourself is a far more important place to start than what to say or do. Each person's experience with dying is an equal opportunity teacher. Every interaction has intrinsic, immeasurable relevance and inspiration for those with the courage to keep their hearts open.

This book is not about spirit guides, psychic powers or metaphysical phenomena. It does not emphasize "stages" of dying or tell you how to help someone have a "good death." *Companioning The Dying* is more about an art form than it is a clinical or theological guide. You will find some companioning philosophy and tenets that I borrow from the teaching and writing of my friend and mentor Alan Wolfelt. You'll be offered enhancements to your listening skills that, when practiced, will help you effectively negotiate your way through almost any situation with the dying. My hope is that the comments and stories I include from my teachers—the dying and their families—become your stories as well.

I will share with you some of the familiar needs the dying often seem to struggle with and ways to honor those needs without taking on the burden of fixing them. *Companioning The Dying* may offer you a different spin on what it means to be helpful. You will hear, in different ways, how emotional, spiritual and existential distress in dying usually masks the very necessary search for meaning. You will be repeatedly assured that being present to one who is dying doesn't ever have to be an emergency. So, if you're a healthcare worker, a volunteer or a family member of someone who is dying, or if you are simply curious about being a respectful companion and these words feel like a relief to hear, this book is probably for you.

I also want to emphasize how passionate I feel that all the paradigms and ideologies published about dying should not be mistaken as formulas or prescriptions to follow. *They only represent a framework through which to view a process, not a final destination!* I find it interesting in reviewing old and new literature on death and dying how around every corner there is an "expert" ready to label—and thus judge—the value of a death as a "peaceful" or a "good death." Does that mean non-peaceful deaths are bad deaths? And do those kind hold less value and potential for learning, wonder and healing?

While I suspect those "experts" don't intend to convey judgment, they nevertheless evoke in me a strong desire to dedicate this book to all the people whose experience doesn't fit popular literary models of dying. (Hand me my soapbox over there…thanks.) What about all the dying people who don't care about spirituality or reconciling their broken relationships…the ones we label as noncompliant, oppositional or in denial? And what of the ones who don't respond to the most well-meaning invitations to investigate the meaning of their life or death? What about all the death experiences that are not peaceful or good or graceful or resolved? Do they hold less value or potential for rich growth and learning for all involved than the poignant ones? Do they deserve less airtime? *Dude*! as my kids would say.

In much of the literature on dying, there is a glaring lack of reference to emotionally and spiritually distressful deaths that perhaps represent less pleasant examples to teach from. And when they are explored, I get a strong impression that those deaths are viewed as less-than or tragic because the one dying was not able to respond to traditional help or in ways offered by the authors. The judgment is veiled, but it's there. The implication is that less poignant, distressful death outcomes, which are many in my experience, are regrettably relegated to the wasn't-that-too-bad category.

I was tempted to subtitle this book, *Honoring All the Clumsy Deaths That Don't Fit Any Popular Models and Nobody Wants*. I personally feel a sense of loyalty and compassion for all those death scenarios that are rough around the edges. Because they tend to be devalued, I feel damned privileged to honor those kind throughout this book.

As helpers to the dying, we're sadly mistaken if we unwittingly assume our least favorite kinds of death experiences offer us fewer gifts or merit less wonder and respect. For me, some of the most complicated, painful experiences in companioning the dying have blessed me the most, with life-changing gifts.

My hope is that you, too, after reading this book, may be less quick to label experiences with the dying as good or bad, peaceful or distressful, pathetic or poignant, and so on. Each one is simply an ending with its own character containing equal potential for learning, growth and healing, regardless of our feelings about it. Each experience with a dying person deserves to be honored regardless of the emotional toll it takes on caregivers and observers. And further, working with the bereaved, too, over the years has taught me that any grief work left over by families after a death can *always* be worked with, no matter how complicated.

One thing that I am convinced of, however, is that whatever one's travel to death looks like, may it be protesting, yearning for God, or gracefully seeking welcome relief from suffering…no individual or group has a franchise on the secrets of that wondrous Mystery. It is exclusive to no one, compelling to everyone and we all belong to it.

Part 1

Companioning Basics

Chapter 1

Tenets Of Companioning

1. Companioning is about honoring all parts of the spirit; it is not about focusing only on intellect.

2. Companioning is more about curiosity; it is less about our expertise.

3. Companioning is about walking along side; it is less about leading or being led.

4. Companioning is more about being still; it is not always about urgent movement forward.

5. Companioning means discovering the gifts of sacred silence; it is not about filling every moment with talk.

6. Companioning is about being present to another person s emotional and spiritual pain; it is not about taking away or fixing the pain.

7. Companioning is about respecting disorder and confusion; it is not imposing order and logic.

8. Companioning is about going into the wilderness of the soul with another human being; it is not about thinking you are responsible for finding the way out.

What is Companioning?

Not long ago a movie was released called *Gone in 60 Seconds*. It dealt with car thieves who could supposedly steal any car in less than a minute. It occurred to me that that movie title also describes people at parties after I tell them what I do for a living.

"So, what do you do, Greg?"

"I'm a hospice counselor. I companion the dying and their families."

"Oh…wow, isn't that a hard job? I don't see how you do it. I could never do that kind of work…but I'm glad there are people who can…Say, will you excuse me? I see someone I need to speak with."

Bam! Gone in 60 seconds!

Supporting the dying, bereaved or any vulnerable population is not something our grief- avoiding culture usually wants to talk about. As someone who is very familiar with this public reticence, I find myself constantly searching for new language that is both accurate and inspiring to describe working with the dying.

In his teaching and writing, author and bereavement counselor Alan Wolfelt has articulated a model that he calls *companioning* bereaved people through loss. I have borrowed from his "tenets of companioning", which beautifully correspond to support for the dying and their families as well the bereaved.

In his book *Dying Well*, Ira Byock, MD, wrote, "While I may bring clinical skills and years of experience to the task, ultimately I am simply present, offering to help and wanting to learn." Companioning the dying is far more about *a way of being in the presence of* than "how to" techniques, methods or clinical expertise.

Companionship begins with a journey inward, looking at our own discomforts and attachments to outcomes. It means valuing the manner and style in which every individual finishes his life without expectation that his experience fit any particular definition of a "good death." Companioning is void of judgment. It celebrates diversity. Every single experience with dying is a highly valued, one-of-a-kind story.

To an observer, companioning looks more like listening than talking. Make no mistake, however; companioning the dying includes being present in ways that the casual observer will never know. Companions recognize and honor emotional and spiritual suffering not as an emergency to be "treated" but more as a kind of compass giving direction to our side-by-side, uncharted walk with the dying.

Helpers who are grounded in the tenets of the companioning philosophy increasingly find that what to do and what to say are not a problem. Companions learn that to create a fertile ground for healing, it is far more important how you are inside yourself while in the presence of one who is dying. Equally important to the dying and their families are answers to the many clinical questions relative to the disease process. However, those finding their way through dying are often comforted the most by those unafraid to stand in the fire with them—without judgment, advice or expectation, regardless of what role they play. The dying yearn to feel adequate and acceptable through something they've never done before. They long for *companions*.

It is with humility that I've learned that regardless of what you, I, or anybody else does, says or thinks, dying people will find their way to the finish line with or without us! Some die introspectively, preferring solitude. Some struggle in distress while others leave this world reconciled with grace and equanimity...but they do leave.

Terminally ill people and their families frequently benefit greatly from our contributions. They sometimes welcome guidance, sometimes not. Their fears and concerns may be eased, their "business" concluded (perhaps with our help), their physical comfort needs addressed, but the fact that *their life will end* is not contingent on our support. They truly don't need us to die. Thus, opportunities to companion the dying strike me as a very special honor. I repeatedly feel blessed when invited to share that most intimate time to make my contribution, whatever it is. Unimaginable things happen for the open hearted. We are always privileged guests in the dying experience of another.

As we understand companioning at deeper levels, we become freed from the illusion that our job is to prevent existential suffering. When our belief system about dying begins to change, we become less apt to interfere with what is already progressing as it is supposed to. Companioning requires buckling your seatbelt and holding on. The terrain is often bumpy, with steep drop-offs and sudden turns. The journey sometimes moves very fast and sometimes imperceptibly slowly…but I invite you to be patient and not judgmental.

If we allow the tenets of companioning to challenge our old definitions of helping, we will be less likely to unknowingly sabotage the reconciliation work of those we are actually trying to support. As we next go through the tenets together, don't be afraid to use your colored highlighter or to write in the margins.

Chapter 2

The Value of Telling Our Stories

God made man because he loved stories.
— Isak Dinesen

Gerald was dying at home, attended by his wife and two daughters, when he asked our hospice to send a counselor. He had earlier been visited by his priest, which was helpful, yet he was still disturbed. As I sat with him and his family, I learned that Gerald was deeply troubled about a memory of bullying a little boy when he was a child.

Judy, one of his daughters, was clearly agonizing over seeing her father so sad and remorseful. She had been relentlessly trying all morning to convince her dad with her best arguments that he was forgiven from any past misdeed. Gerald, however, remained haunted by his memory and it was tearing Judy's heart out.

In their presence, I invited Gerald to tell me the story of his bullying. Judy immediately interrupted, challenging his guilt, discounting his need to "fully own" his past behavior by telling his story. I asked Gerald to continue and Judy was quiet. I tried to model, allowing Gerald to have all his feelings about his experience without expectation he do anything for the moment. He needed to reinvestigate and wrestle with his memory and past behavior without pressure or judgment from others.

I asked, "Gerald, if you could somehow get a message to that little boy today, what would you like him to know?" There wasn't a dry eye in the room as he conveyed his deep sadness about his behavior and asked the little boy, wherever he was, for forgiveness. I mused out loud how important it is that we all feel permission to remain engaged in the process of reconciling personal dilemmas. Gerald needed backing from those who loved him to feel as sad as he really felt. He needed to tell that story again, after which he became very quiet and said our time together was helpful.

As I was leaving, Judy and I stood in the doorway and I offered my observation that forgiveness toward self or others is really grief work. It's a process, not an event, and in finding reconciliation with being wounded or wounding another, one needs to travel through all the feelings caused by the experience. One needs to tell the story and feel the story. Only then can mercy for self or others become authentic. I've never observed forgiveness-on-demand work for anyone.

I credited Judy for how much she loved her dad and how hard it was to see him hurting over this or any matter. I invited her to view her father's angst as what his work of healing looks like. I felt privileged to teach Judy a little about companioning philosophy while modeling it for her.

In his book *Hymns To An Unknown God*, author and teacher Sam Keen includes a chapter beautifully entitled "Autobiography: Your Life as Sacred Text." In it he tells part of his life story, inspiring the reader to explore and honor sacred meanings in their own. He reminds us that each of our lives is a sacred text worthy of investigation and discovery. And further, every single life story is an essential part of a greater epic shared by all mankind. Recollecting personal history and telling our stories forms the narrative that makes each life a once-told tale.

In my wildest dreams I could never imagine having more love for the uniqueness of each of my own children's life stories. How about you? Without the contribution of every single life story, from your family to mine, including the dying we companion, the universe would be forever incomplete.

Most people facing death find it relieving and healing to tell their stories. Many are eager while others respond after gentle, curious invitations. Others still are reluctant, even in the presence of the most compassionate listeners. Companions have the patience to honor the rate of speed at which one is able to embrace a frightening reality.

Stories may represent what is happening at the moment for the dying person or family member. Perhaps the story is about changes in their disease process. Their story is this life and everything happening in it. It is the sum total of their past as well as dreams or fears of the future. Every person represents the sacred text of their once-told story still in progress.

Those dying tend to review their lives for meaning. Author and researcher Dr. Robert Butler articulated this phenomenon as "the life review" process. Companions recognize the importance of bearing witness to these stories. We can share our wonder about the significance of reawakened memories by taking forays down memory lane. Our curiosity for details allows the dying to reflect on past and present times with the possibility for new wisdom or at least validation that their lives were meaningful.

A slice of my story

I remember getting a new pair of cowboy boots when I was about six. Proudly walking out the door to school, I ignored warnings from my folks about new leather being stiff and nonsense about blisters, blah, blah, blah. Halfway home from school that day, I prayed for Jesus to fly me the rest of the way because my feet hurt so badly. I sat on the sidewalk and waited for a rescue that didn't come. I had to tough it out. I learned that day that cowboy'n can be a hard life. Since then, I've been just close enough to working cowboys to confirm that truth.

Fact is, I'm a wannabe cowboy. That's no secret to those who know me. Roy, Hopalong, Gene and all the other silver screen and TV cowboys are quietly my heroes. Like a lot of boys in the '50s, I was smitten. For a long spell, my mother tells me I wore my toy six-guns and holster to bed at night…wouldn't take them off for anyone. The cowboy code states that no one touches another man's guns. My mother tried only once at my bedtime, but I threatened to wing her and she backed off. She was a lucky woman that night.

Fate saw fit not to birth me into a ranch family, but I still wear boots, own a couple hats and sport a handlebar mustache. I drive a pickup truck, have been on a few round-ups and have a passion for Westerns. In college, I learned to play the guitar, which has been my faithful companion ever since. I carry one behind the seat of my truck and as the American Express slogan says, "I never leave home without it". (Don't you hate it when you need a guitar and don't have one?)

For years, I have utilized music in companioning the dying, their families and children. It has been inspiring beyond words and left me with many heartwarming stories. I hope the poem of mine on the following page helps you understand.

In recent years I have found myself writing and playing more western music and poetry. In part, I credit my dad, who played *Sons of the Pioneers* albums around the house when I was growing up. Their rich vocal har-

The Hollow Box

Behind the seat of my truck it sits
In a canvas zipper bag it fits
A Hollow Box, strings, pegs
Reverberates the sound of music made

Touching the ears of young and old
Both the healthy and the sick who are sadly told
Their time is short, Sit with me, they say
I unzip the bag and begin to play

This Hollow Box against my breast
Gives joy to some, to others rest
Tears are welcome as much as laughter
But what transpires in the moments after

The music stops is so revealing
The reflections that follow, the spontaneous healing

Healing not of the physical type
You know, the kind that gets most of the hype
But a subtle healing in the secret heart
Inspired by the music may kindle a spark

Of understanding healing from a broader scheme
What a lovely helpful life-changing theme
So even during loss there s hope for restoration
Made possible, in part, by this collaboration

Which note for you animates a restless sigh
Of memories past and days gone by?
Do they come in tones, rhythms and nomenclatures
Or is your music unlike that defined by some other nature?

Seems our melodies have such different faces
Diversely shared in times and places
I guess I believe every heart composes an original score
You mean no one ever thought of you as musical before?

Well believe it! However you convey yours
Either common or rare
It can simply be enough to know it s there

Somewhere in a greater cosmic space
Where all wondrous melodies first take place
Now echoes through my chambered heart to test
This Hollow Box against my breast

A Box that beckons when I m away too long
For a ballad, a lullaby or a children s song
An entire universe of notes cry, choose me, choose me
Until I caress the strings, and set them free

monies, lively tunes and enticing cowboy stories told through their music awakened in me a passion that remains strong today.

Throughout the west and southwest we have what are known as cowboy poetry and Western music gatherings. They're becoming quite popular. Authentic working cowboy men and women (and wannabes) gather to recite what is actually quite sophisticated, beautiful, and often humorous poetry and to sing music on western themes. It's good family fun and keeps the heritage of the American West alive.

Throughout this book, I have included some savvy sage from the old west, in the form of quotes here and there. The purpose for these one-liners is to compress the bigger lesson into a colorful takeaway phrase.

Chapter 3

Active Listening ("Old Reliable"):
Where the rubber meets the road

"Never miss a good chance to shut up."
— Ken Alstad

Certain memories stick with all of us. Especially if the experience was frightening. As a kid, I tended to be on the quieter side in the classroom, reluctant to ask questions. I can trace some of my reticence back to an experience in the first grade. This would have been around 1958 or '59 in a little town in southern Colorado.

We had a rather large, looming elderly teacher who was not particularly memorable except for one incident. I remember sitting somewhere in the middle of the class one day at my desk, bent over a worksheet, when the boy sitting next to me went into violent convulsions. I saw his arms fly up in the air, flailing all about while his head was jerking back and forth as though it could snap right off at the neck.

To my horror, I realized he was not having a seizure, but our teacher had quietly tiptoed up behind the boy, who was apparently goofing off, gripped him by the shoulders and was shaking the hell out of him. Mrs. Looming was screeching while she worked, "I…told…you…to…get…to…work. Young man, I think the devil's got a hold of you…"!

I thought I heard him say, "I…think…she…has…too…"!

I nearly wet my stamps. The whole class was frozen with terror. Today, of course, there would be CAT scans, hearings, dismissals and perhaps abuse charges filed. But back then I must say she got the desired result. Traumatizing, yes, but there wasn't any fooling around in her class.

Now, I don't know about the other kids, but there was no way on God's green earth I was ever going to raise my hand in her class again. What if she was having a bad day and I answered wrong? I loved my head and didn't want it snapped off at the neck. Instead, I compensated by becoming an even more acute listener. I've always been stronger at listening than at volunteering thoughts openly, thanks in part to Mrs. Looming.

One of the best pieces of advice given to me when entering graduate school was to volunteer on a crisis hotline. That I did, and got some of the best training and practice in active listening I could ever imagine. It was even better than my Counseling 101 class in graduate school. Over the years I have refined those skills and added others of course, but "old reliable" continues to be my most valuable companioning tool.

The art of "joining" through active listening

Active listening helps us do the work of joining people where they are at any given moment. When people feel joined or accepted, they will more likely feel safe to disclose important things, to tell their stories. "Old reliable" helps us become effective listeners and joiners.

Following are the four key elements of active listening:

1. **Attending behaviors** include eye contact, facial expressions, openness with posture and sometimes appropriate touch. Our body language can perhaps convey more of a sense of acceptance than any other manner of active listening. It can also give away discomfort in both subtle and overt ways.

   In graduate school when we were practicing our listening skills, we did an exercise where we paired off with a classmate. One would share a life experience while the other listened, then we would reverse roles, finishing with feedback to each other.

   My partner, Rena, shared the story of the death of her young daughter to a childhood disease. I thought I was doing quite well, listening, making eye contact, showing sincerity in my facial expressions—but this is the feedback Rena gave me. "Greg, the closer I got to the actual moment of my daughter's death, you began leaning away from me. Your body turned to the side in your chair and you shifted positions as far from me as possible without actually getting out of your chair and leaving." (I had no conscious awareness this was happening. I was lost in her story.)

   Rena continued with her most helpful and painful feedback. "As a bereaved mother, if this were not a classroom exercise...I would have stopped telling you my story a long time ago. I could see how uncomfortable you were becoming." Ouch!

From then on I began going inside myself, checking out my own response to being in the presence of others who are suffering emotionally. Certainly it's not bad when we're touched by another's loss, but the important learning for companions is to be aware of our own feelings while we attend others through painful life transitions.

People facing loss want to know if those around them can tolerate the flames and not be afraid or back away as I did with Rena. Our attending skills are one of the most powerful ways we convey our willingness to not back away.

2. **Paraphrasing** is another active listing technique. It amounts to saying back to another what they have just told you, but in your own words. It confirms to the speaker that you indeed are hearing them and just to prove it, will give back what was just said.

Sam: "The last few months have been so hard. I've been passed around from doctor to doctor. Each one tells me something a little different and none of them are talking to each other."

Greg: "Wow, so you've been a bit like a ping-pong ball bouncing from office to office with no one doctor coordinating all the input."

Sam nods affirmatively and continues his story.

3. **Reflecting** is another active listening feature. It is like holding a mirror up to another and offering back the *feeling* you hear behind their words. This can help them check with themselves what they might indeed be feeling but that may not have surfaced in their consciousness.

Mary: "Being laid up here in rehab with a broken ankle while my husband is at home dying is terrible. I hate it!"

Greg: I'm sorry, Mary. You sound angry finding yourself in such a helpless fix and I'm guessing very sad, too."

If I'm right, Mary may continue her story and do a little grief work.

4. **Clarifying** is important to make sure we understand the exact meaning of something unclear. It confirms to the speaker we don't want to misunderstand even one small detail.

Daniel: "I'm not afraid of dying. I have a strong faith that comforts me. I'm more afraid of what might happen between now and when I die."

Greg: "Do you mean you're afraid of being in pain or how your body might change? Help me understand, Daniel, what specifically you're afraid might happen."

Old Reliable is very forgiving. If we guess incorrectly when reflecting or paraphrasing, those we companion will correct us. That's what is great about joining through listening. We aren't afraid to get it wrong because having our misperceptions corrected by those we companion even further confirms our dedication to not wanting to miss anything important.

Old Reliable is a way of honoring exactly where a person is at the moment. Active listening techniques convey no judgment and no expectation for change. They liberate companions from having to solve, fix or save someone from their hurt. Isn't that a relief? Active listening is the bread 'n butter of companioning work. Even if we have only a few minutes at a time to spend with people, we can create trust and join faster by actively listening than anything else. During extended conversations, companions can practice active listening in between pertinent information that may also need to be presented regardless of our role.

For every disciplined companion who can actively listen, there are 50 other well-meaning helpers just waiting in the wings to spill their guts with all their solutions to *resolve* the spiritual, emotional and existential dilemmas of dying. Companioning, on the other hand, practices trust-building more through patience and good active listening. Skillful active listeners are gifted, wise and, I think, quite rare. May we all become one.

What active listening is not

Active listening is n o t

offering solutions for their problems.

emphasizing interpretation or explanation of another's experience.

giving them answers to spiritual, existential or philosophical questions.

giving advice or constructive criticism.

trying to comfort with popular euphemisms like: God never gives you more than you can handle. or At least you ve had a long life.

(Unless, of course, one first volunteers the euphemism as their philosophy).

"Good death"—what does that mean?

Most of us who support the dying carry a mental picture of what we would consider a "good death." Our criteria may include scenarios with loving family, finished business, spiritual reconciliation and the absence of emotional and physical pain. I daresay all of us would wish for a peaceful death for ourselves and our loved ones. It is a wonderful thing indeed if a byproduct of our companioning contributes in some way to what appears to be a meaningful experience for the dying. However, I fear if we're determined that those we support meet our picture of a good death, we run the risk of manipulating someone else's dying experience for our own personal comfort reasons.

So, what happens when our "good death" criteria don't come to pass? Does the experience then become a "bad death" and is it then less valuable? Could not the experience still hold meaning and richness? Could it hold the potential for learning and insight for both the dying and those who love and care for them? Can the experience still stretch us in ways we can't imagine, even if it's painful? Aren't the adjectives we use to describe death scenarios really a commentary of personal expectations and discomfort with differentness?

Celebrating individuality and honoring self-determination is the foremost work of companioning the dying. The dying and their families teach us there is nothing more important than maintaining integrity with one's own values, philosophy of life, and style. The more rigidly we hold to "good death" definitions that qualify or assign value to the dying experience of another, the more we risk distancing ourselves from those whose choices are contrary to our picture.

Companioning means authenticating a dying person's unique style of living, dying and discovery along the way. Certainly we may invite the dying to consider the implications for their choices. And as companions, we may share observations based on what seemed helpful for others who have died, but we cannot be overly invested that anyone conform to traditional values or textbook authority. Whatever an end-of-life experience looks like, it is befitting all the circumstances that bring the experience to this moment. The style each person chooses to manage his death always has much to teach us here in earth school.

Therefore, it seems presumptuous to me—perhaps even arrogant—for anyone to promote the language of "good death" without carefully qualifying it as personal opinion. So, when we read about or hear others speak of "good deaths," we're just learning about where that individual places import and value.

As companions to the dying, we wish that every death experience would be patient-honored, patient-directed and free of physical and emotional suffering. They're not, of course. But every dying experience still has value and potential to awaken insight and healing (in both the one dying and the helper), regardless of how graceful or tragic it appears. Your and my thoughts and feelings about another person's experience with dying in no way adds or detracts from its intrinsic value. Deaths are neither good nor bad in my opinion…just befitting the complex variables surrounding them. We can choose to look for meaning or not. It's up to us to keep our hearts open to what the experience may hold for us. I don't know about you, but I don't want to sleepwalk past the potential gifts that await me, regardless of how distressful it may be to hang in there.

Part 2

Tenets Of Companioning

Chapter 4

Tenet 1
Companioning is about honoring all parts of the spirit; it is not about focusing only on intellect.

*"A wise cowhand will have something
'sides a slicker for a rainy day."*
— Ken Alstad

I realize for centuries theologians have written volumes on the nuances of spirit, yet I shall still offer to you my wannabe cowboy turned companion-to-the-dying definition of spirit. Our spirit might be broadly described as our nonphysical essence, which may include dimensions such as intellect, emotion, personality and spirituality. This tenet has to do with a dying person's meandering back and forth from their head to their heart, between intellect and feelings.

Those of you with experience in supporting the dying will recognize how many people facing death seek protection from the surprising intensity of emotion by intellectualizing their experience. Though this may represent one way of coping, the one dying risks disenfranchising herself from precious parts of her own spirit, resulting in a kind of death long before her heart stops beating. Being careful not to judge, companions can respectfully invite the dying to teach us more about those less familiar, often less comfortable parts of themselves where feelings and passion reside.

Intellect: just one part of spirit

Grace was a retired chemical engineer, newly diagnosed with advanced metastatic disease. In her mind, she carefully calculated each unfolding bit of information from doctors and other consultants who interpreted blood tests, scan results and physical exams. She also listened to the opinions of loved ones, who offered their most encouraging spin on each piece of emerging scientific data. Grace relied on her intellect to guide what became a personal crusade to research her disease and gather more facts and statistics on curability. Throughout her career, intellect had been her closest ally and successful problem-solver. It also led her mission to search out ways to reverse her condition and prolong her life.

It seemed as though Grace needed all available information on her case, but she had to begin experiencing undeniable physical symptoms before she could justify her prognosis and embrace feelings about it. It's an understatement to say intellect is invaluable. Intellect has inspired the genesis of industrial and technological revolution beyond our wildest dreams. However, dying is as much grief work as it is fact-finding or understanding science.

Dying includes saying goodbye to the world, one's self, loved ones and all the attachments to earthly things that hold meaning. For companions, honoring the spirit means inviting the dying to revisit all that has gone into making them the people they are. As companions to the dying, we are acutely aware of becoming better acquainted with the being inside the body to which a disease has attached itself.

As companions to the dying, we are acutely aware of becoming better acquainted with the being inside the body to which a disease has attached itself.

Human bodies are indeed the primary vehicles that transport spiritual beings around the earth. The wannabe cowboy in me, by the way, wishes I could make home visits on a horse. But the last time I rode one was on a round-up in southern Wyoming. I had what cowboys call a wreck, falling off my horse and ending up in the emergency room. Alas, I now transport myself around in a 1990 Dodge pickup. It had a transmission transplant recently and I was reminded that while both machines and human bodies are miraculous things, eventually they all go bad or wear out.

The dying often identify more with their deteriorating bodies than with other dimensions of their spirits. Companions understand that the dying are infinitely more than their physical anatomies. There may, however, be a stockpiling of grief about how the body that once served them so well is failing. Admittedly, I'm pretty darned attached to my body, too, but for those patients who may rely only on using their gifts of intellect for coping, we can lovingly and curiously invite them to teach us about other aspects of their spirit.

How might we recognize spirit?

Companions might recognize evidence of spirit in the form of passion for any aspect of life, such as love of music or art, for example. For Grace, I listened for expressions of love for people, work, or the value she placed in relationships. Her interest in religion and philosophy taught me something about what also had inspired and sustained her throughout her life. I learned more about her spirit through her reverence for nature and animals. We identified and honored her devotion to chemistry, sense of humor and playfulness, which were also parts of her spirit.

Intellectual understanding of disease process first helps people begin to deal with the reality of what they are facing. Desperation for facts is common. But finding one's way to a more reconciled state of mind before leaving this earth almost always includes something more. It means having other important dimensions of spirit recognized, validated and honored by self and others. What a wonderful gift when companions can join the dying on such a fieldtrip.

As companions, we can rely first and foremost on our curiosity and listening skills to guide us as we learn from the dying, the real experts in their experience. We can recognize and credit the beauty and tenacity of intellectual understanding. And being considerate of their comfort level to do so, we can invite dying people and their families to investigate and speak from their heart, from their feelings, from their spirit.

Chapter 5

Tenet 2

Companioning is more about curiosity;
it is less about our expertise

"If you find yourself in a hole...stop diggin."
— Ken Alstad

There's an old cowboy saying that goes, "Good judgment comes from experience, an' experience comes from bad judgment." When I was first hired as a hospice counselor, I was proud to lend my "good judgment" to that needy population. At the request of other clinical experts, I dutifully marched into homes and inpatient rooms trying to subtly awaken patients out of denial into acceptance.

I quickly learned that being too attached to our own expertise can leave us estranged from the very people we are there to serve. I began to see that whenever a patient or family member took too long struggling with a frightening new reality, we simply labeled them *resistant* or *in denial*. Very convenient for us, demonstrating our expertise while keeping a judgmental finger pointing at their character flaws. We'll just send in the counselor to change them! (By the way, how many counselors does it take to change a lightbulb? Only one, but the light bulb has to really want to change!)

I have to say, I'm not necessarily impressed with long credentials, years of education or claims of expertise by helpers of the dying—that is, unless they're seasoned with a strong sense of humility and willingness to learn. Though helpers may have practical knowledge and experience, I have the most respect for those who defer to the dying as being the true experts in what they're going through. Tenet Two invites all those enthusiastic care providers who often can't wait for an opportunity to share all their knowledge to listen more with curiosity before speaking out.

Certainly, companions to the dying have valuable information and observations to share. But for creating safety in relationships, curiosity can be more important than our expert guidance, explanations, interpretations or advice.

Our curiosity opens up meandering pathways on which to walk with the dying. Even if they feel lost or without direction, the more they talk, the more we learn, and the more we learn, the more of their story we have to ask questions about. It's my experience that every dying person will give us what we need to know to adequately support them. What guidance we do offer will then likely be more sensitive to the nuances of their characters.

Even though I'm a very different kind of counselor today, at times I still find myself overly attached to my "expertise." Berta's unwillingness to acknowledge she was dying made it difficult for her to understand the rationale for adjusting her medication and need for more daily care. Her hospice nurse asked if I could help in any way.

As Berta shared her story with me, I had no expectation that she should be any different than she was. I only wanted to learn from her. Yet before leaving, I couldn't resist offering her some of my great wisdom—based on my expertise, of course.

"Berta, you've helped me understand how important it is for you to keep your energy focused on healing your body," I said, "Your survival instinct has helped you overcome so much in your life. I also know from experience how it is a relief to talk about these things with a good listener."

"Actually, it makes it worse," Berta replied. "I don't find it helpful at all to talk about these things."

Oops. I realized if I would have remained curious and asked, "Are you the kind of person, Berta, who finds it helpful to talk about your disease and what it means?" she would have told me no. So much for my expert assumption. I had forgotten for a moment that she was the expert on her dying, not me.

The Mystery

Kim was 32 years old and dying of colon cancer. He said to me one day, "I would gladly become the most wayward, homeless street person just to stay alive. I so badly don't want to leave my family. Why do people with so much to live for have to die?" He could find no satisfactory explanation. A part of me felt pretty helpless at the time, as we searched for a way to tolerate this dilemma. I did my best

"Nobody but cattle know why they stampede…and they ain't talkin'."
— Ken Alstad

Teach Me

Curiosity works well with a teach me model of questioning. Often the dying or their family members will ask, Well, how do we begin? or What do you want to know?

I like to be curious, with big, open-ended questions. I m here mostly to learn from you. Can you teach me what it s like to be in your shoes right now?

The old actor John Houseman once made a television commercial for the investment firm Smith and Barney. His line was, They make money the old fashioned way they earn it. I feel so strongly that companions to the dying, too, should only have the right to offer guidance the old fashioned way they need to earn it. We earn it through curiosity, through first asking many questions. We earn the right to offer guidance by doing our homework, allowing each person to teach us about what it s like to be going through his or her ordeal.

It s been said, As long as we believe we have something a dying person needs, we can never be for them what they truly need us to be. Our investment that they receive this need we have for them will always get in the way of us being a curious empty space wherein they can safely search for meaning without pressure.

to just honor our not knowing. It was hard for me; I couldn't imagine what it was like for Kim.

Science may be able to provide partial answers to explain the complexities of disease pathology, but with every mortality issue, there will always remain lingering questions about randomness, timing, circumstances and causation. The Great Mystery will likely always be part of the equation.

Information lubricates mental gears, allowing them to more smoothly upshift and downshift over the uneven landscape of a changing reality. I will always encourage companions to become more familiar with our para-doxical human nature, which simultaneously searches for answers while desperately trying to figure out what to do with "not knowing." This dichotomy is present in almost every single issue with the dying and their families. Everything in life, actually.

With hospice patients and families, I often refer to The Mystery as a place to temporarily suspend the unknown. It's comforting to me to treat it as a kind of sanctuary, lovingly safeguarding all the yet-to-be and perhaps never-to-be revealed answers. The Mystery welcomes both casual knocking and desperate pounding on its door. It cradles the secrets of life and death while celebrating our need to do the asking. For the dying, their families and those of us who companion them, feeling permission to visit the troubling questions over and over may be as therapeutic as finding answers. The search is meaningful.

Not knowing what the dying experience may hold is understandably dis-tressful. Sharing information learned from other dying people is some-times helpful. Yet, everyone needs to intermittently rest and water the horses when facing a frightening reality. Mercifully, companioning philoso-phy liberates us from any urgency to force one to face reality. Remembering that denial and magical thinking protect us against the full impact of what initially seems unbearable, companioning calls for non-judgmental understanding of these responses and patience to match. A new reality will form in its own time.

As patients struggle with The Mystery, the need for creating metaphorical containers to hold the unanswerable questions becomes important. Containers could be thought of as beliefs or practices that provide a work-ing explanation, even temporarily, for the most troubling dilemmas. Containers help us to function in the face of life-changing events.

Never has our country so searched for philosophical or spiritual containers than after the 9-11 terrorist attack on New York City. We all watched in shock as interviewed rescue workers, families and media tried to find ways to hold the futility of such an insidious act. Thousands volunteered time, money, blood and prayers as a way to combat helplessness. Each of those actions represented containers helping victims to temporarily hold what was incomprehensible. Remember comments tearfully made by loved ones awaiting news about missing family? "You have to appreciate what you have" and "Never miss an opportunity to tell your family you love them" were among them. These comments reflected some of the philosophical containers in which to hold The Mystery surrounding that trauma.

Long ago, Granny Lee gave me a deeper reverence for The Mystery. She was 95 years old and caring for her 70-year-old daughter, who was dying of end-stage Alzheimer's disease. "A parent should never have to bury a child," she told me, "no matter how old they are." Granny baked a cake and was preparing to bring it over to the hospice house to honor her child's 71st birthday the next day. Her daughter died that evening, just before her birthday. Granny brought the cake and left it with the staff anyway.

I made a visit afterward to Granny Lee, who still lived independently in her own home. When I invited her to tell me more of her story, Granny tearfully disclosed that she also had buried a 3-month-old daughter more than 70 years ago. Shaking her head, she mourned both these losses 70 years apart as we sat at her kitchen table. Though the timing of her own children's deaths remained a Mystery, she didn't protest much. In her 95 years, Granny Lee had become well-reconciled to the cycle of life and death as a reality. She had seen plenty. Almost a century of life experience represented a pretty solid container in which Granny held these two profound deaths.

As we talked, she conveyed a kind of acceptance, perhaps even reverence for, The Mystery that inspired me. I felt such gratitude to both support Granny Lee and to learn from this wise and wounded woman. In some ways, she was the Zen Master and I was the "grasshopper."

For my money, the concept of companioning partners nicely with The Mystery. Companions are prepared to pause with the dying as they may temporarily idle in neutral, immobilized by the unknown. Or we may honor their need to backtrack, frantically looking for answers around washed-out roadways of hope. No matter which highways or back streets the dying travel, honoring The Mystery can help liberate us from an urgency to always find the right answers. Companioning the dying never has to be an emergency.

Chapter 6

Tenet 3

Companioning is about walking alongside; it is less about leading or being led

"Ride the horse in the direction it's goin."
— Ken Alstad

Every person approaching death walks through the experience at her own pace. For some it seems steady; for others, the tempo changes. Physical symptoms, environment, personality, age, life experience, and spirituality might impact the rate of speed and timing at which a dying person will reckon with emotional or existential dilemmas. Companioning requires speeding up, slowing down or standing still, but all the while remaining shoulder-to-shoulder, side-by-side, in our walk with the dying.

From our first meeting, Mrs. Scott loved to muse about philosophical and spiritual dimensions of life and death. We seemed to march at a steady, conversational pace as we discussed topics from after-death possibilities to reincarnation. A little curiosity on my part went a long way with Mrs. Scott. She kept the momentum rolling with her own curiosity and found it inspiring to explore the "Great Mystery." As with almost all dying people, her walking tempo changed as her disease weakened her. At times, we walked at a very slow pace. yet she still found it rewarding to have a companion to join her daydreams, if even for a brief spell.

Walking alongside means having no judgment about whether or not the dying choose to explore emotional, spiritual or family issues. Unlike a "treatment" model of care, companioning does not push, pull or lead patients to a prescribed mindset so that their death experience more closely fits a textbook example. Walking alongside is not about gratifying the expectations of healthcare workers.

Janelle was dying of lung cancer. Hers was a family plagued with generations of abuse, chemical dependency and dysfunction that make the Ozzie Osbourne family look like the Cleavers. Janelle requested counseling from our hospice—reportedly to find some reconciliation with her somewhat estranged daughter, Julie. It didn't take a rocket scientist to quickly learn that her request was only a ploy to enlist enforcement to help shame Julie into moving in and serving her as an indentured slave.

When we met together, Janelle and Julie instantly launched into an attack on each other, pointing out what a poor excuse for a mother or daughter each had been. They shamed and persecuted with equal enthusiasm. It was clear that neither of them demonstrated an authentic interest in—nor had the skills to take mutual ownership of—longstanding, discordant issues. Generations of abuse and family wounds found expression through anger and reciprocal blaming. With the limited time Janelle had left to live, the best they could hope for was to coexist on superficial but civil ground to keep the environment less hostile. I suggested they seek support separately to dialogue about sensitive issues that became uncontrollably explosive in each other's presence.

The reconciliation they had postponed until Janelle was dying turned out to be an illusion. For these two, it was more important to be right than to be in relationship. For a companion to walk alongside would never be satisfactory to them. Each wanted to lead and attack. This mother and daughter would have used any well-meaning helper as a club to beat down the other into submission. When I wouldn't play, they had no use for me. Companioning of high maintenance people requires good supervision, clarity of role and conscious boundary setting. It is very easy to get triangulated into the swirling vortex of multigenerational, untreated pathologies. You'll recognize these people and environments as they very quickly make you feel crazy or unsafe. I find it helpful to debrief experiences like this, in confidence, with wise and trusted mentors.

Companioning of high maintenance people requires good supervision, clarity of role and conscious boundary setting.

Walking with the dying means to invite (and the key word is always to *invite*) others to teach us about what seems important in their end-of-life walk. With curiosity from others, the dying will often investigate more than they would otherwise. But when they become uncomfortable with the topic of conversation or pace, companions honor their need to slow down, rest or change topics. After all, this is their walk. We are the privileged guests.

Walking alongside means crediting the distance and pace walked together as meaningful *regardless of whether we can immediately see results or not*. My experience has been that most dying people and their families (unlike Janelle and Julie) respond very positively to being walked with. The value in companioning lies perhaps not so much in what may be readily identified as meaningful; it just may be more important that we were simply joined in relationship with the dying person for a period of time. As a companion to the dying, I often get the impression that ours is the closest thing to unconditional acceptance they have ever experienced.

What could be more healing, when you think about it? We convey to them that we value their presence without condition. We're not afraid of what they are facing and bring nonjudgmental acceptance to their state of mind, choices of heart and condition of body. For companions to the dying, it can be liberating to remember that it is never our mission to lead the dying to some destination—because we already honor them as existing in a state of adequacy. Thus, we respectfully walk alongside them. What better environment could there possibly be for a dying person to do whatever he needs to do?

Chapter 7

Tenet 4

Companioning the dying is often more about being still; it is not always about urgent movement forward

*"If yer ridin' ahead of the herd, take a look back
every now and then to make sure it's still there."*
— Ken Alstad

Whenever possible, I encourage companions to enter each new relationship with the dying from a place of stillness inside themselves. Allowing ourselves to slow down inside, while focused on listening, helps us to hold a moment with little or no anticipation for something to happen. Companions may then trust that the dying will initiate their own movement, direction, rate of speed and final destination. It's their show.

John was a Vietnam vet who lived in a nursing home. He was disabled and dying of emphysema. Shortly after the war, he estranged himself from his family, including two children. For years, John used alcohol to cope with the effects of combat trauma. During the last few years of his life, he was able to maintain sobriety and spoke often and with pride of his grown children and grandchildren, whom he would hear news about from a brother every few years.

Periodic urging from nursing home staff members who had grown to love him did not convince John to reconnect with his family. He quietly rejected their well-meaning suggestions of creating journals, taping his thoughts and regrets, or writing letters. His shame and inability to forgive himself was too great. John chose to bear his losses while being sustained by pride in children he didn't even know.

At his memorial gathering, I listened as those who cared for John shared their respect and admiration for his kind heart and friendship. They voiced regrets that he never was able to find reconciliation with family and so many personal demons. In their heartfelt words, I could hear how hard it was at times to be still in the presence of John's emotional pain and choice-making. The gathering seemed to help those who loved him not judge the end of John's life by values other than his own.

Companioning the dying has taught me that staying in relationship is far more important than trying to manufacture a good death. If we can remember that companioning does not have to be an emergency, then feeling permission to be still in the presence of one dying will come more easily. It's OK to feel like there's no movement toward resolving philosophical or spiritual issues. If we have a sense of urgency that the dying find acceptance or reconciliation with something or someone, our expectant energy will likely get in the way of us being for them what they truly need us to be. The dying (and all people actually) are sensitive to the slightest pressure or judgmentalism.

For companions who are overly invested in outcomes, being still might be difficult. The tenet of being still challenges the old saying, "Don't just stand there...do something!" Being still inside often means, "Don't just do something...stand there!"

I've noticed that for every dying person who does find some reconciliation with estranged relationships or internal dilemmas before she dies, there is someone who doesn't. It bears repeating that companions *invite* the dying to take a step toward what may be important to them, but in the spaces between our invitations, we can practice being still, listening and accepting with no urgency. Yet, in fairness to us all, practicing stillness is not always easy.

The good people who cared for John in the nursing home remind me how hard it is, at times, for companions to be still inside. Honoring the dying without a sense of urgency to be moving toward an idealized ending takes patience and practice. When I companion the dying within a framework that esteems each life as already existing in a state of adequacy (regardless how peaceful or distressful it looks), I'm more apt to honor each person's death as being sufficient. It was the best they could do based on their complex history and what they had to work with. I wish I could say I'm always able to maintain that awareness. I'm not, but I like myself so much better when I do.

Divine Momentum

It's darned complicated being a human being. In dying, each person brings with them a collaboration of generational, cultural, biological and social conditioning. Spiritual or religious practices also provide some framework. giving structure and meaning to an existence that might otherwise seem futile. Suffice it to say, there are infinitely more influences at work in our lives than we can shake a stick at.

"If you follow a new track, there ain't no way a-knowin' if the one who made it knew where they was goin."
— Ken Alstad

It also seems probable to me that all these contributions are parts of a more sacred intention—a collaboration with our Creator, if you will. The result is *Divine Momentum*. It has to do with what author Sam Keen calls "the dance between freedom and destiny." Divine Momentum is perhaps the music that inspires the dancing. It is disguised in the flow of everyday life. And though we sometimes feel lost or stuck without direction, life doesn't stand still waiting for us to figure it out. Unabashedly, without judgment, life is never static, never misses a beat. It moves forward with loving indifference. For it has Divine Momentum.

For me, the word Divine is broad enough to transcend descriptions of God that purport to define how God thinks, feels, plans and behaves. (Traditional definitions always seem exclusive and limiting to me.) A more elusive, mysterious, yet merciful and loving version works best for me. The word "Momentum" indicates motion of both physical and nonphysical experience. It reinforces that we are free to make our contribution to the dying knowing we are not responsible for shaping or fixing the outcome. We can listen, be curious, help them investigate and search for meaning. We may then stay or leave, trusting Divine Momentum will continue to propel the dying to an inescapable yet always valuable death.

I sometimes liken Divine Momentum to having a letter from a mythical merchant princess who grants passage through a most exquisite but perilous countryside. No promises exist for safe travel. In fact, no one comes through unscathed. But Divine Momentum assures us that while the Observer is not there to rescue us, Her limitless love and support are always felt. I do think Her silhouette may be visible on the horizon from time to time, however.

For me, mindfulness of Divine Momentum encourages me in several ways when I am companioning the dying:

1. *Companions are liberated from the tendency to value the details of a dying person's experience as good or bad, finished or unfinished, reconciled or unreconciled.* Honoring Divine Momentum helps dignify every part of the dying experience as being important. Nothing is wasted. Divine Momentum reminds us that every dying person is always in a state of adequacy, regardless of how obnoxious or obsequious they may be. Certainly, as companions we have our most and least favorite aspect of participating, but that's a matter of our own personal comfort.

2. *We are freed from feeling that we possess something the dying person must have.* As long as we believe we have something the dying can't live without, we can never be for them what they truly need us to be. In other words, urgency to present our agenda will obscure our line of vision to their heart. It will interfere with us being a neutral, empty space in which the dying can meander in their search for meaning. Paradoxically, any gifts of companioning we may offer the dying are important yet not critical to the completion of their dying. Divine Momentum will carry them to their deaths, with or without us.

3. *Honoring Divine Momentum helps us know the timing for change or healing is not dependent on our companionship.* Though companions often make a signifi-cant contribution to the dying and their families, we serve more as a cat-alyst for something to happen rather than the party responsible for it. It frees us from the illusion we are more powerful than we really are. We add our offering to that of thousands of others who have influenced the one dying somewhere along the way. Eventually, a person dying transforms not because we hit the home run with our profound coun-sel, but because we lend ourselves to the mix, then step back and honor the rate of speed at which meaning surfaces. Every unfolding moment, therefore, becomes a win-win proposition.

Having respect for Divine Momentum reminds me we are truly making a cameo appearance in a storyline already in progress. We honor those we support however we find them. They have no choice but to be in a neces-sary state of being, culminating from their own unique evolution of social, familial and spiritual influences. How could it be any other way?

My encouragement to companions is to actively listen, be present without judgment, offer practical assistance to the dying and generally practice the Tenets Of Companioning as best we can. Then we may trust that all we observe—the thinking, the feeling and the doing—is floating on currents of Divine Momentum, right before our eyes.

Chapter 8

Tenet 5

Companioning the dying means discovering the gifts of sacred silence; it does not mean filling up every moment with talk

*"A man can learn a heap of things
if he keeps his ears washed."*
— Ken Alstad

My closest friend, Peter Woods, also a hospice counselor, tells one of my favorite stories about the importance of sacred silence. Late one afternoon, he walked into the room where Mrs. Green was resting quietly in bed, not far from death but still conscious. Recognizing Peter from an earlier introduction, she reached out her hand as if to greet him with a shake and closed her eyes. The two gripped hands, with no words spoken. Recounting the story, Peter recalls having not been compelled to offer any words.

"I cannot animate with breath, sylla-bles in the open mouth of death."
—John Peale Bishop

Mr. Green also sat near the bed, silently greeting Peter with a nod. Peter described feeling awkward at first, but decided to just trust that something important was happening in the absence of audible words.

The scene remained unchanged for 10 or 15 minutes, when Mrs. Green finally relaxed her grip, hand falling back to her side. Her eyes did not open, nor did she make any other gesture toward Peter. Mr. Green also remained silent and reflective. Peter admits it was initially uncomfortable, but he closely watched those two for signals to verbally engage them. Sensing none, he found himself nodding and quietly leaving the room without exchanging any words. Mrs. Green died a few hours later.

Peter's story grew more fascinating when he bumped into Mr. Green a few months later.

"Hey Peter, I'm so glad I ran into you!" said Mr. Green. I wanted to thank you so much for what you said to us on your last visit." Remembering clearly he had said nary a word, Peter was most intrigued. "What was that, Mr. Green?"

"My wife and I both found a great deal of comfort when you asked her if she was ready to go home." For a brief moment, Peter thought about assuring Mr. Green he had not spoken a word, but thought better and just accepted his expression of gratitude.

Peter and I have often marveled at his experience, which inspires me to trust the value in silence more when companioning the dying and their families. Even though no words were actually spoken, nonverbal messages were making their way back and forth. Peter had the wherewithal to remain silent and not disturb the Divine Momentum. His presence and conduct were sufficient to convey acceptance and support. He resisted any urge to disrupt the moment by trying to say something poignant, and t*he Greens heard exactly what they needed to hear!* I find that so cool! (I guess Peter made a *mute* point.)

During meaningful dialogue, periods of silence may allow people to slow down inside. Chatter or too much talking without breaks can disrupt one from formulating or reviewing important thoughts or to simply hold emergent feelings. I would invite each of us to be more conscious of any personal discomfort that builds during silence. We might ask ourselves, "Is my breaking the silence with more talk or questions meant to assuage my own discomfort, or does it truly seem needed at this moment?"

Companioning the dying means stretching our capacity to hold silence, remembering it is far more important to know how we are inside ourselves with what's happening than what we say or do.

At a gathering to honor hospice volunteers, a young woman named Jenny shared a memorable story that taught me much about sacred silence. She had only been a volunteer a short time and was sitting with a dying elderly woman. At her bedside, Jenny was touching her hand while the woman rested quietly without apparent distress. As the moments passed, Jenny described herself as becoming more uncomfortable with the silence. Feeling compelled to say or do something, she finally leaned close to her patient and asked, "Would you like to pray?"

The slight figure roused long enough to tilt her head toward Jenny and say in a weak voice, "Sure honey…if it'll make you feel better."

Chapter 9

Tenet 6

Companioning is about being present to another's emotional and spiritual pain; it is not about taking away or fixing it

"A good friend is one who rolls their own hoop."
— Ken Alstad

Perhaps the most difficult of all tenets to understand and practice has to do with the important role of hurt in healing. For most people it is unbearable to be in the presence of another's emotional or spiritual distress without being compelled to ease it. Most of my life I "helped" people by distracting or minimizing their emotional pain. Like many, in my desire to be helpful I did my best to lead people in the opposite direction of their necessary, legitimate expressions of grief. No one ever taught me that emotional and spiritual pain must be free to flourish before it can subside.

Our culture has little understanding of this truth. Relative to others in loss, we have the fastest euphemisms in the west, meant more to assuage our own personal discomfort than address the sufferer's painful reality. Ever notice how we stop people from grieving at our discomfort level? Once in a while our well-meaning euphemisms are helpful, but often they're reported as insulting. Here's a few I have either heard or used before I knew better:

"It could always be worse."

"You're not really losing your children; you'll be their angel."

"At least you got to be their mother for eight good years."

"Remember, God never gives us more than we can bear."

"Everything will be OK…really."

"Well…God has a reason for everything."

Gradually, helping professionals are learning that mourning an anticipated loss necessitates tolerating painful feelings and finding safe expression for them. To me, the hallmark of a wise companion is her ability to courageously honor emotional and spiritual hurt for its therapeutic value without feverishly trying to make it go away. The dying have taught me how existential heartache lessens all by itself when cradled in the arms of acceptance. This is a radically different notion of helping than I was raised with. How about you?

In his book *Care Of The Soul*, author Thomas Moore reminds us that "Melancholy gives the soul an opportunity to express a side of its nature that is as valid as any other, but is hidden out of our distaste for its darkness and bitterness."

He continues, "Often our personal philosophies and our values seem to be all too neatly wrapped, leaving little room for mystery. Depression (spiritual and emotional pain) makes holes in our theories and assumptions, but even this painful process can be honored as a necessary and valuable source of healing."

Companioning people through their end-of-life journeys has shown me over and over how all those intense feeling associated with grief create openings through which people gain insight and find transformation. Their change is observable partly through their expressions of relief, release from fears and more reconciled feelings about dying.

Shelley celebrated her 35th birthday in our hospice house. She was heavily medicated but able to tearfully describe how sad, angry and guilty she felt that God would have given her such a beautiful daughter three years ago and now was taking her away. Heart disease was preventing her from being the mother her daughter needed and she resented that someone else would raise her. Her internal suffering was visibly agonizing. A part of me wanted to take Shelley in my arms, rock her, and tell her everything would be all right. But it wasn't all right. I was aware that a part of me wanted consoling. However, at that moment, Shelley badly needed me to validate and accept without judgment feelings she felt were shameful and could not share with anyone else. I became a collaborator in the reality that her terrible dilemma was real. Together we honored her authentic feelings, exposed in a moment of implicit honesty and intimacy. It turned out to be liberating for both of us.

Shelley expressed her gratitude and I could see some transformation in her as she relaxed and fell quietly asleep. My own tears caught up with me later about how the experience affected me, but I felt blessed to be part of the necessary chemistry that actuated a moment of mourning and healing for Shelley. Her existential pain was not futile pain, it was meaningful pain—the kind of pain that leads to the relief of pain. Get it?

Her existential pain was not futile pain, it was meaningful pain.

When people ask me, "How can you do what you do?," I think, "How could I possibly convey with words the depth of gratitude and level of intimacy that come with moments like the one with Shelley?" So, I just say, "I'm in it for the money."

Seriously though, one of the most paradoxical truths in all human services work deserves repeating throughout this book and it is this: *spiritual and emotional pain is a necessary part of healing, albeit in its most distressing disguise.*

Companions understand, too, that to tolerate what is frightening and painful in others, we have to be on tolerable terms with our own grief. In fact, we have to be regular, active grievers. In some ways, we share universal tears, being members of what Helen Keller called "the great family of the heavy-hearted into which our grief has given us entrance." I would invite all companions to remember that emotional and spiritual pain is not the enemy.

Chapter 10

Tenet 7
Companioning is about respecting disorder and confusion; it is not about imposing order and logic.

"Some cowboys got too much tumbleweed in their blood to settle down."
— Ken Alstad

Shep Wallace lived in a 24-foot travel trailer that looked like someone threw a grenade inside. He drank a quart of whiskey each day and for our hospice team, managing his metastatic cancer pain was a challenge, to say the least. Shep had difficulty following the directions on his medications, ate crappy meals (the opposite of happy meals) and was becoming a safety risk. He was barely a phone call away from obliging us to contact to Adult Protective Services. But he was contented with his lifestyle and rather resented intruders. Shep had no use for goody-two-shoes social workers or counselor types. Disorder and confusion was his middle name. He was, nonetheless, a likable character who lived independently. Like Shep, his death was also self-directed.

Terminal illness doesn't discriminate. It shows up in all families, from the most healthy, adaptive ones to the most chaotic, lower-functioning ones. Dying is an event that disrupts balance, forcing family members to reschedule their lives. Financial and emotional resources may quickly become depleted, increasing stress. Emotions intensify. The advent of terminal illness almost always creates some amount of disorder and confusion.

Yet I can't help but notice that those dying as well as those who care for them tend to have some illusions about how dying should unfold in a systematic, organized way. Well, hey…when was *anything* in life ever that way? Dying is often hectic. There is drama. There is sometimes an unconscious positioning for control among whomever is the neediest—caregivers, family member or the one dying. Responding to the complex interaction between physical care needs, lifestyle disruption and feelings of grief can be a circus of disorder and confusion. The obsequious ones who are sweet, compliant and well-organized in their dying are in the minority. In general, I'd have to say that the dying experience is usually pretty hard work with plenty of rough edges.

Cases like Shep always stretch our hospice team to review our role as responsible care providers while being respectful of the dying, who have every right to live in disarray, drama and confusion. Many of those we companion never completely understand how to utilize the hospice team. They never find reconciliation with the fact that they're dying. They remain angry, protesting, questioning God, struggling for some reason to have hope in anything. Companioning means understanding the need for the dying to experience disorder and confusion as a necessary part of their search for meaning.

Misunderstanding this central truth contributes greatly to burnout among those who feel called to care for the dying. Dear readers, disorder and confusion is just wrapping paper on an important package to be opened by the dying. That's not to say they won't find their own way to some clarity and serenity as a result of our support; often they do. But we must be equally OK whether they do or they don't find peace! Otherwise we'll always be banging our heads against the wall trying to control their experience, stuck in helper's prison, with no way out.

One of my chosen mentors is a little Albanian woman who, in Calcutta, India, companioned thousands of dying in an environment of disorder and confusion. In spite of surrounding chaos, Mother Teresa was perfectly clear that her job was essentially to love the one she held in her arms at the moment. The outcome, she once told a skeptical reporter, was up to God. She loved them to death. This humble Nobel Peace Prize recipient, addressing a group of religious mystics and physicists in Bombay, once said, "We can do no great things; only small things with great love."

"We can do no great things; only small things with great love."

As companions to the dying, we respect how disease pathology can play havoc with body chemistries, creating unusual and moody sensations that can indeed be frightening and distressful to the one dying. It can be confusing to understand if a patient's changing behaviors and perceptions are due to menacing disease erosion, powerful medications or psychological and spiritual struggles. In fact, I think I'd be very curious if a dying person wasn't at least a little discombobulated at times.

I would invite us to think of companioning as liberating, not encumbering. I try to remember there's no such thing as an emergency. We may need to repeat the same information many times to the dying and their families. We may answer the same questions over and over in different ways while they're trying to absorb a fearful new reality. Companions may need to offer constant assurances and be flexible in how we provide our particular service. And we need to be OK if patients never completely feel organized, resolved, reconciled or settled about their leaving this world. Some do; many don't.

Whether your role is professional, volunteer, friend or family, remember there is Divine Momentum. Hold on, open your heart and don't freak if the actors in the drama mess up their lines, rehearsals are late or the set designs catch on fire. Really...who cares how well-organized or logical one's chronicle of dying looks and sounds? It's their story.

To all those rigid helpers who try so hard to choreograph a neat and tidy death scenario, I offer the reminder that neither internal disorder nor environment confusion is an indicator of *value*. For every single moment in one's dying, regardless of what it looks like, holds rich potential for insight, growth and healing. So, take some deep breaths and buckle your seat belt a little tighter. Like Mother Teresa, our job is to hold that one right there in front of us (whatever that means in our role) and try to detach from outcome.

Everything belongs

I've shared with you how mindfulness of Divine Momentum grounds us with confidence that our companioning of the dying harbors a complex network of meaningful influences. And making room to honor the Mystery allows us to treat the "unknowns" with greater reverence. But, possibly the most poignant axiom of companioning is trusting that *everything belongs*. While I aspire to this noble mantra, it is the one with which I agonize the most.

"Even a cowchip is paradise for a fly."
— Ken Alstad

A belief that *everything belongs* suggests to me that once we have an experience, regardless of its nature, our challenge both personally and as companions is to reconcile its membership to the sum total of all else that has happened in our life. We have to bring it into the fold, so to speak. We must ask ourselves, "How does this belong in all I know about how the world works?" No matter how we suffer or protest a life event, it can never *not* be a part of our life, now that it's occurred. So it is that, in this context, *everything belongs*.

This principle does not suggest to me that everything must be *welcomed* or that we even need to find "acceptance" for it. It does not judge or minimize our protest and personal suffering in its wake. It simply means we're tasked with searching for a modicum of meaning in all things. Rudy, a young soldier, we'll read more about later, said in language consistent with his combat experience, "This cancer is kickin' my ass!" Though it was never welcome, this career soldier found a context of belonging for his cancer as his most battle-worthy adversary to date.

"God would never let my dad die. I know he's going to get better," thirteen-year-old Justin said to his mother. Justin's father, Jerry, suffered greatly as his cancer worsened. With love and support from his family, Justin could finally measure with his own eyes the inevitable truth he was facing. After a long protest, this young lad was able to carve out a place of belonging for his father's death in the form of merciful "relief" from his suffering.

For those of us who are dedicated to alleviate suffering, *everything belongs* can be especially difficult. It invites us to ask, "What important thing might I take away with me from this experience? How is it my teacher?" But when stressed, the impulsive response of goodhearted caregivers is more like, "You can take your learning and stick it!" When our minds protest being pulled outside our comfort zones, it becomes nearly impossible to companion the dying in areas outside of theirs. Does that make sense?

Inviting helpers to look for "belonging" in painful experiences is very lonely work at times. In fact, even talking about this paradoxical truth is uncomfortable for most people. As helpers, we must understand how embracing hurt, though it feels rotten, stimulates the forces of healing. Hurt *belongs* in this way.

For me, *everything belongs* is different from what many faith traditions relegate to a catchall category of "God's will" or "God has a reason for everything." Those phrases suggest intentionality behind our losses, which has never been a comfort to me as one who grieves nor has it given me hope in my companioning of others. In fact, it angers me.

Harold Kushner's writing has been a comfort to me in suggesting that our losses are mourned by our creator as well. In his book *When Bad Things Happen To Good People*, he states,

> Let me suggest that the bad things that happen to us in our lives do not have a meaning when they happen to us. They do not happen for any good reason which would cause us to accept them willingly. But we can give them a meaning. We can redeem these tragedies from senselessness by imposing meaning on them. The question we should be asking is not, 'What did I do to deserve this?' That is really an unanswerable, pointless question. A better question would be, 'Now that this has happened to me, what am I going to do about it?'

Nature and humanity run amuck at times and tragedy happens. When it does, we can choose to search for a context of meaning...or not. But we are forced to accommodate what happened into our working reality of the world. Fortunately, we're endowed with the ability to grieve and mourn, a process that helps people eventually find a place of belonging or reconciliation toward our losses. My greatest learning in companioning the dying and bereaved has come from the cases in which my heart ached the most.

John Walsh had to accommodate a place of belonging for the murder of his young son, Adam. He produced the television series *America's Most Wanted*, which for years has led to the arrest and conviction of hundreds of perpetrators. In spite of his pain, he continues to create meaning from his loss through making the streets safer for our children. With every arrest, he honors his son, Adam. I have great admiration for Mr. Walsh.

Because our grief-avoiding culture lacks mentorship in this area, I can understand how looking for a place of belonging for advertisity is difficult. Therefore, developing a philosophy that looks upon suffering with mercy instead of disgust is necessary if we're to walk with people through their losses with equanimity. We will find ourselves talking less about "good" or "bad" deaths and more about honoring all elements of the dying person's experience as belonging somehow. We will value the infinite possibilities of growth and healing regardless of how peaceful or painful an experience appears. With greater conviction, we will begin to say, "Everything belongs."

Chapter 11

Tenet 8

Companioning is about going into the wilderness of the soul with another human being; it is not about thinking you are responsible for finding a way out.

"A stone stops rollin' when it finds the kind of moss it wants to gather."
— Ken Alstad

In the literature and customs of every culture in the world can be found rituals meant to discover spiritual truths. Religious pilgrims make trips to Mecca. Native Americans have practiced the custom of going on a vision quest. The teachings of our greatest spiritual leaders from Jesus to Buddha have emphasized the importance of making literal or metaphorical trips into the *desert*, the *wilderness* or up to the *mountain* in search for the secrets of life and death or enlightenment.

Though some of us do plan actual trips to remote regions of the world, most of us take inward forays, agonizing with life questions while we go about day to day life. I've often thought that dying must be the ultimate vision quest. Although you and I have the opportunity to companion the dying to the doorway of that pursuit, it is still life work that the dying must do themselves. When I find myself thinking about companioning others into the wilderness of the soul, I also think about the nature of paradox.

As companions, I would invite each of us to develop our understanding and practice of honoring the paradoxical nature of all things. The American Heritage Dictionary defines *paradox* as a seemingly contradictory statement that may nonetheless be true. Paradox exists in all things at all times.

Chemotherapy, for example, may arrest growing cancer (good) while at the same time having some treacherous side effects (bad). No one chooses their terminal illness (bad), yet some make reconciliation with others and find meaning in life they never imagined they could (good). Before he died of AIDS, actor Anthony Perkins described how he turned his adversity into meaning, finding unexpected growth and healing he wouldn't have traded for anything in the world. "Out of our ashes come our greatest gifts," I heard poet Robert Bly say at a conference.

So it is that when we more deeply accept the paradoxical nature of life and death, we can be more merciful toward all the ways of seeing the world differently than our own. Things in life become less good or bad, right or wrong, welcome or unwelcome. They simply hold multiple meanings depending on where we stand or how we are at the moment. Right?

Going into the wilderness of the soul with another means walking with them through spiritual or existential crises without judging the agony of their search as a bad thing. As companions, we're challenged with one of life's great paradoxical enigmas: how we are at the same time both universally connected and immutably separate. We are connected, say, in our shared humanity and in our dependency on one another for emotional, spiritual and familial support. In many ways we structure our communities to foster safety and connection. When one of our children meets with disaster, every parent mourns, so deeply bonded are we in our humanity.

But paradoxically, we are also immutably separate from all other human beings. For example, no one can grieve our losses but us. No one can bear our personal pain for us. Not one other person can take away or stand in for us when it's our turn to die. Though companions can walk beside another into the wilderness of the soul, no one but no one can supply us our meaning or provide an escape route for a way out of dying. There are always plenty of goodhearted codependent caregivers who give it a try. But no one can walk our walk through dying for us…but us.

Understanding this paradox seems much more difficult for caregivers than for the dying. People facing death often appear to have a better grasp of their separateness in the context of this paradox. Though they sometimes rely on magical thinking or denial in hopes of reversing their dying, out of the many hundreds I've companioned I can't remember any who have ever asked me or someone else to trade places with them. Plenty of loved ones, however, have offered to trade places with the dying if they somehow could. But for the dying, there seems to be an innate reconciliation of this one reality: we each must do our own dying. If companions, too, recognized this predisposition, perhaps we would be less likely to lead the dying away from the wilderness of the soul.

So, how would we recognize helpers with an urgency to rescue the dying from the wilderness?

1. They may be too quick to distract with answers and explanations for wilderness dilemmas.
   - "Don't worry, God has a plan for you."
   - "Just focus on the good things you've accomplished."

2. They may over-comfort with assurances that "everything will be all right."

3. They may minimize one's grief or the emotional importance of asking existential questions. "I know you're scared or sad, but we can't question God's plan. He knows what He's doing."

4. They may interfere with a dying person's natural tendency to own and express their feelings, agonize with tough questions or protest reality.

Walking into the wilderness of the soul with another human being means leaving our expectations and road maps at home. Companions are not tour guides nor are we members of a rescue team. We buy one-way tickets, wear comfortable walking shoes and pack our active listening skills, which validate the experience of others. Whatever language used to describe the deeper spiritual regions of dying, be it *wilderness of the soul*, the *desert*, or the *unknown*, companioning is far more concerned with *being in relationship* than with destination or outcome.

Chapter 12

Step lightly Oh Gladiators,
Among the delicate flowers,
Desperately placed near subjects fallen
By their beloved, to mitigate the hours

Cultivated in rain and drought
In league through mystic years,
Their garden yields those tender stems
An offering of love and farewell tears
— G.Y.

Companioning vs. Treatment:
An important distinction

In a November 2000 *Time* magazine article, Dr. Sherwin Nuland wrote of medical students, "Modern medicine is action; its excitement comes from the challenge to intellect, to technological skills, even to personal daring. The greatest victories go to those who diagnose brilliantly, who are undaunted by the most intimidating confrontations with disease, so long as there is a possibility of cure or at least improvement. *These are the biomedical gladiators.*"

Alan Wolfelt reinforces how important it is to honor emotional and spiritual pain without trying to change it. As the director of The Center for Loss and Life Transition in Fort Collins, Colorado, Dr. Wolfelt speaks and writes extensively about how the traditional medical model of care, conditioned to "treating" grief-related issues, is not effective for that purpose.

The way health care is conducted today, many of those who practice medicine unfortunately have little time or interest in the emotional and spiritual distress of patients and families. When they do address them, they tend to treat responses to loss as pathological, maladaptive coping or as something broken that needs fixing. Dr. Wolfelt points out that the word treat is actually derived from the Latin *tractare* which means literally "to drag or pull."

Emotional and spiritual distress relative to dying is not a mental illness. It is not maladaptive coping that requires dragging and pulling. An existential dilemma is not a symptom that needs managing. Skin breakdown, nausea and infections respond to treatment. Metastatic bone pain and physical discomfort need to be treated. But unless it's debilitating, the emotional and existential distress that accompanies one's end-of-life experience is not the enemy.

Medication can tranquilize the feelings associated with one's internal struggle to reconcile dilemmas, but only temporarily. Indeed, for some, medication used judiciously can sometimes take the edge off anxiety enough for companioning to be effective. But as companions, I feel we are tasked with de-pathologizing the necessary role emotional distress plays in the dying process.

At our best, companions recognize there is usually nothing to treat relative to emotional and spiritual matters. However, for more complicated cases, such as severe depression, debilitating psychological diagnoses, or tendencies toward self-harm, intervention and more aggressive treatment is called for.

At our best, companions recognize there is usually nothing to treat relative to emotional and spiritual matters.

The feedback I receive from physicians, nurses and most healthcare workers overwhelmingly indicates that making the philosophical shift from "treating" or "fixing" a patient in emotional distress to companioning them represents a huge challenge to their strong conditioning as "biomedical gladiators." Nurses, especially, convey how companioning alone feels woefully inadequate when supporting terminally-ill people with internal angst. Medical model conditioning compels us to do something to make it go away.

Hospice is unquestionably the best game in town for understanding and providing care for the dying. Important advances are continually being made in the art and science of pain and symptom management for dying patients. Yet hospice, too, has far to grow in understanding and practicing the distinction between treating and companioning nonphysical needs.

Nearly all hospice physicians conduct a major part of their practice in the curative care culture. Many hospice patients themselves maintain at least some connection to aggressive medical care for non-hospice related needs. Most hospice personnel have been well-steeped in curative models of care for years before arriving to work at hospice. I regularly observe how, at a moment's notice, even hospice workers are quick to offer patients a solution or strategy to solve dilemmas that mostly need acceptance and someone to walk with during the struggle. Helpers are often uncomfortable with this important process. It is always helpful for me to be reminded that emotional, spiritual and existential angst represents reconciliation in progress.

Honoring the struggle:
A challenge to treatment

Western medicine is quite uncomfortable with disruption in homeostatic balance. Medication is readily available to alleviate distress that most counselors would consider normal in legitimate feelings of grief. Patients demand it and physicians are often uncomfortable with expressions of intense emotions. There is little teaching or encouragement for honoring spiritual and emotional struggle as life's way of inviting us deeper into the Mystery. Inspiring the search for meaning through adversity is not a priority in health care. Companions are encouraged to value the tensions created by end-of-life challenges. But when the pot gets stirred, my friends, even though it's uncomfortable, the tension that follows inspires movement, exploration, questioning. It energizes the search for meaning!

Perhaps our greatest contribution as companions comes in the form of joining, referred to in chapter 3. We offer counsel judiciously, inviting others to find their own meanings in our words and stories. But more than our words, it is our very presence as merciful witnesses that allows patients and family members to find their own way into healing. Unlike the treatment model of care, companioning doesn't feel a sense of urgency to make emotional and spiritual distress go away.

Ellie Mae

"So, what is it that you think you can do for me?" asked Ellie Mae defensively.

I picked a chair in her apartment close to where she sat. "I don't know, Ellie Mae, but I can make you this promise. For whatever time we spend together I will never back away or be afraid of anything you need to say about what you're going through. I have no expectation for you to meet and in my eyes you will always be acceptable however you feel or whatever you want to talk about."

Ellie Mae's face softened and her eyes glistened. She took my hand and described how seldom in life she felt that way with another. We both knew that neither of us could reverse what she was facing. It was a moment of reconciliation. We established that she would not traverse this frightening new territory in isolation nor would there be judgment about how she was equipped to meet it.

Permission existed in our dialogue for her to have her anger, fear, and questions, and for her to experience all responses to dying without any urgency to resolve anything. Having been told that I was a musician, Ellie Mae said, "What you can do is play your music for me."

I learned from Ellie Mae that she had a lifetime love of music and dancing. On my second visit I played "Somewhere Over The Rainbow." She swayed gently in her wheelchair, oxygen tubing in her nose, eyes closed the entire time. When I finished we sat quietly for a moment.

"That was my husband's favorite song," Ellie Mae mused, "and while you were playing I was dancing."

I asked her to tell me more about her husband, dancing and music. I learned that from early childhood, Ellie Mae loved to dance and did so at every opportunity. I didn't see my role as being there to fix her depression or give her insightful explanations about her anger or protesting of her disease. When the dying and their families ask for support to investigate those things, I'm ready to facilitate the search. But for Ellie Mae, her reflecting and my listening was the focus of our brief relationship.

Ellie Mae remained angry about her disease but had neither the strength nor the inclination to explore it much. In spite of protesting her death, she did share with me a bit of internal peacemaking she achieved before her death a few days later. Her anger and depression didn't need treating particularly, it needed validating. She and so many like her need to feel acceptable in their struggle.

Ellie Mae died with both anger and angst about her disease, yet in no way was the value and quality of our experience diminished. Ellie Mae's death was neither good nor bad. It was just Ellie Mae's. It was valuable. It was befitting her personality and nature. But like every dying experience, it was predisposed with richness for anyone willing to keep their heart open. Who started the good death-bad death myth anyway?

Ellie Mae's family asked me to sing at her funeral. I felt honored and wrote this song.

Ellie Mae Dancing

Gathered by the fire, in evening attire
The parlor was filled not by chance
Then someone mentioned, without apprehension
Oh, Ellie Mae please won t you dance

Every eye was affixed, on the child only six
Skipping to the center of the floor
Like a small crimson flower, she could dance for an hour
With onlookers asking for more

Dance, please Ellie Mae Dance,
Take us somewhere far away
Waltzing on wings, to the orchestra strings
Give us one more dance today

Won t you dance, please Ellie Mae dance
Whirling about here and there
With Ellie Mae spinning, every face would be grinning
At the dancer uncommonly rare
All the days of Ellie Mae dancing.

Dancing through years, helped quiet the tears
For changes and hardships in store
Yet, she was contented, and no one lamented
With everyone asking for more

When a young man dreams of courtship it seems
Thoughts turn to love and romance
So lucky was he, who was able to be
One with whom Ellie Mae danced

Years later greeting, we found ourselves meeting,
In her room with memories grand
From a well-used wheelchair, she transcended despair
Though her legs could no longer stand

Today she waltzed on the wings of my own guitar strings
Whirling about in her mind
And for a moment at least, the world seemed at peace
To the dancer uncommonly fine

Oh dance, please Ellie Mae dance
Take us somewhere far away
Waltzing on wings, to the old guitar strings
Dance just one more dance today

Won t you dance please Ellie Mae dance,
Whirling about in your mind
And lucky for me, I was able to be
One with whom Ellie Mae danced
All the days of Ellie Mae dancing.
In the last days of Ellie Mae dancing

Humor belongs, too

I'm convinced that humor ranks among the most important of all human virtues and is at the very center of our spirituality. Humor does so much more than relieve stress; it is an indicator of another paradoxical truth promising that opposite the expressions of sadness and hurt is the reward of joy, laughter, humor and healing. The degree to which we embrace one corresponds to the degree we can experience the other.

Humor follows expressions of self-mercy and forgiveness. Aren't we silly about what impossible standards we hold ourselves to? We can find thousands of ways to laugh at ourselves. We can laugh with compassion at how absurd we all can be. We're reminded that what is so funny in others we find as true for ourselves. Humor is essential in practicing palliative companionship work. When I begin taking myself too seriously, I snap a pair of underwear on my head and look at myself in the mirror. Try it sometime. It's a form of "brief therapy."

Levity, wit, and play counterbalance the heaviness of what is often painful in life. Humor represents an oasis of relief from the hard emotional and spiritual matters consistent with companioning the dying.

About the word myth

Myths have historically represented ancient stories that teach about cultural mores and ideology. While the characters and tales are fictional, the psychological and spiritual themes are often full of truth and usable teaching for everyday life. When we use it today, the word myth, on the other hand, may imply a half-truth or even a completely untrue assumption.

It could be said that our entire belief system about death and dying is our personal mythology. But in the context of this book, it seems right to me to specifically associate mythology with non-concrete, paradoxical concepts such as denial, letting go, good or peaceful deaths and stages of dying. There must certainly be both truth and fiction in the knowledge and practice of these themes.

Therefore, whenever references are made in this book to myths or mythology, please know that I mean for personal truth to be searched for in the story or theme. I don't mean myth to be viewed as a falsehood unless otherwise noted.

Treatment vs. Companioning
For Spiritual, Emotional and Existential Issues

Treatment Model	Companioning Model
To return to original homeostatic balance.	Honor present circumstances as important. Welcome a "new normal."
Control or stop distressful symptoms and behaviors efficiently; distress is bad.	Accept and honor distress as important to the healing process.
Follow a prescriptive model to assure a good death outcome. (Road map provided.)	Patient guides the journey. Honor every outcome with equal value. (Uncharted territory, no map provided.)
Outcomes range from successful to unsuccessful, from good to bad.	All outcomes are valuable, rich in learning.
Quality of care judged by how well the situation was controlled.	Quality of care measured by how well we allowed the patient to guide.
Patients and families range from compliant to noncompliant.	Patients and families express their fear differently, and cope as best they can.
Denial interferes with efficient delivery of services. It must be challenged!	Denial represents the rate of speed one moves toward a frightening reality. It is matched with patience and compassion..
Success measured by how well all problems were resolved.	Having provided responsible, patient-guided care, every ending is adequate.
Every patient and family eventually need to let go.	"Letting go" is a self-determined process. Not our job to mandate.
Establish control; agenda comes first.	Show up with curiosity; join first.
Healthcare workers are the experts.	Patient are the experts; they will guide us.
Noncompliance, resistance and poor coping are a bad reflection on me.	My self-identity and esteem are not contingent on how patients respond to frightening end-of-life experiences.
Supply satisfactory answers for all spiritual and emotional questions and dilemmas.	Defer to patients for their own wisdom; honor the "Mystery;" no urgency to to solve or satisfy the dilemma.

Part 3

Mythologies

About the word myth

Myths have historically represented ancient stories that teach about cultural mores and ideology. While the characters and tales are fictional, the psychological and spiritual themes are often full of truth and usable teaching for everyday life. When we use it today, the word myth, on the other hand, may imply a half-truth or even a completely untrue assumption.

It could be said that our entire belief system about death and dying is our personal mythology. But in the context of this book, it seems right to me to specifically associate mythology with non-concrete, paradoxical concepts such as denial, letting go, good or peaceful deaths and stages of dying. There must certainly be both truth and fiction in the knowledge and practice of these themes.

Therefore, whenever references are made in this book to myths or mythology, please know that I mean for personal truth to be searched for in the story or theme. I don t mean myth to be viewed as a falsehood unless otherwise noted.

Chapter 13

"Letting Go" Mythology

I grew up around the construction industry. My dad was a contractor and a gifted craftsman, passing many of his skills to me. I learned to frame homes, drywall, roof and trim them as well. For a time, I had my own wood shop building cabinets and custom furniture. During that part of my life I often wore a leather tool belt. Attached to it were pouches in which I kept such tools as a tape measure, nails, pencil, chalk line and hammer. Under pressure from my wife, I still get them out occasionally for domestic improvements. (Her favorite line is, "Wouldn't it be nice if we moved some walls and built in some cabinets here?")

When I began working in hospice at the end of 1992, I observed many fellow workers for necessary tools or skills needed for the job. Some had cared for the dying either in hospice or traditional health care for years. As someone new to hospice, I trusted my colleagues knew what a "good death" should look like. What I found was that some might as well have carried tape measures and pocket watches as they attempted to influence length and duration of patients and families who took "too long" facing reality. For that was clearly the goal. Pry-bars could have helped break their patients' fearful clinging to life, urging them to let go and welcome a more "appropriate," textbook death.

I noticed how a few of my colleagues may as well have been using a ball-peen hammer and steel chisel as they chipped away at their patients' denial. I think bar clamps and vice grips would have been helpful for squeezing noncompliant, highly independent dying patients. Maybe a high-speed drill would have expedited the penetrating of the old-fashioned thinking of families who held on too tightly to their dying loved ones. A saber saw could have efficiently cut through unorthodox tradition. But even without my old construction tools, the determination with which many professionals directed the dying and their families to let go was impressive.

However, those kinds of helper-directed, rigid tactics never felt like how I would want to be treated if I were dying. As I spent time with dying patients and their families, they began to teach me how disenfranchising those rigid expectations from helpers could be. The dying began to teach me that instead, detachment from outcome, nonjudgmental acceptance and patience with one's style and timing was much more helpful to receive. While things have improved some, many professionals who care for the dying are still under the hypnotic spell of academic pedagogy that suggests the clinician is the expert. It is a model that implies a "good" or "bad" death is measurable by compliance with a plan of care.

It's been my observation that too many who care for the dying are occupied with people letting go of one thing or another. I hear helpers complain that a dying person won't let go of his fight for life or the illusion that he's not as sick as he really is. Family members either won't "release" their dying loved ones or else they plead with them to let go and end their suffering. Letting go advice is popular with well-meaning helpers who themselves are uncomfortable with the dying person's emotional roller-coaster ride to death. To me, any urgency we convey for letting go risks minimizing the complex attachment human beings have with one another and to life. Advising one to "let go" may be more about convenience for the helper. It essentially means, "Please do it my way." Really, now—who's the one with the problem?

Hidden within letting go words I hear, "I'm getting tired of how long it's taking you to accept this dying business. Everybody would be greatly relieved and much less troubled if you would get with the program and just accept the inevitable." Letting go advice oversimplifies process-oriented grief work. Reconciliation with dying is a pretty big deal. It just can't be legislated on command.

Anyone who has ever facilitated a bereavement support group will agree that a familiar theme discussed by members is feeling shamed by the public for grief that is taking too long. People experiencing loss are very sensitive to community intolerance for what they need to do the most…tell their story, over and over. I'm sorry, but letting go advice has little or no place in companioning the dying.

It's not uncommon even for experienced hospice workers to give letting go directives to family members and patients. For example, I occasionally overhear compassionate helpers offer their one-size-fits-all speech to family members about how they need to "go in and tell your mother (or loved one) that it's OK to let go." In my early days of companioning, I was eager to inform families of their duty to let go and give their dying loved one the same admonition. Vice grips and pry bars worked well for me.

One of our biggest challenges as companions is to "let go" of our investment that others let go.

Self-check questions for letting go advice

Fellow companions, when we're tempted to offer the loved ones of a dying person the "You need to tell him it's OK to let go" speech, let's be sure of a few very important things:

1. We've done the diligent work of learning about the history and nature of the relationship between patient and family members. We're comfortable a letting go message would be consistent and respectful of their family culture. Remember—we are in the presence of vulnerable people whose experience here may likely impact them the rest of their lives.

2. We're certain that any instructions are appropriate to the context of the particular situation. For example, do we know for a fact the visible distress or lingering of the dying person is really about needing permission to let go? Are we certain it's about unreconciled relationships or spiritual distress—or is there the chance it could be physical or neurological responses to disease or pain? Is the non-responsive patient possibly a survivor who knows only how to keep fighting, familial or spiritual issues notwithstanding? Could her lingering be about something else entirely? (Honestly, how can anyone truly know these things?)

3. Before we offer our thoughts, we have allowed the family to first offer theirs. We have encouraged the family to say anything they can think of that may be helpful to their dying loved one to hear.

4. We've discussed with the family the possibility that the patient may in fact die soon after their letting go words—and helped them foresee how they might feel about that. Or, if the patient doesn't seem to respond to the letting go words, how would that be?

5. We've reviewed our personal motives and are not attached to any timetable a patient may have for her process of dying. We trust there is meaning for the patient in the timing of her last breath.

More than a few times, I have met with bereaved people who have painfully regretted being told by a well-meaning helper to tell their loved one to "let go." They did so against their better judgment. "It didn't feel right," the daughter of a patient once told me. "But I did it because people who regularly work around the dying are supposed to be the experts." She felt guilty and ashamed for not trusting her own intuition. Letting go words were not appropriate to their relationship but the care providers did not investigate these issues before giving letting go instructions.

Another woman named Louise asked for a counseling visit after her husband died in our hospice care. She was most grateful for several months of loving care provided by our staff but said she was troubled by something that happened while her husband, Sandy, was dying. "What was that, Louise?" I asked.

"A couple days before Sandy died, one of the nice nurses told me I should go in and tell him it's OK to let go, that he was holding on because of me."

"What happened?" I was very curious.

"Well, I most certainly did not. Sandy and I would never have said something like that to each other. We always tried to be hopeful during hard times. I just went to him and kept telling him how much I loved him, how much I needed and would miss him."

Was Sandy holding on to please or protect Louise? Maybe. Would he have taken that long to die if she had given him permission to let go? Maybe, maybe not. Do people die soon after being told by loved ones that it is OK to let go? Sometimes there seems to be a direct correlation, sometimes not. How can we ever know for sure? I just think one-size-fits-all advice about telling others it's OK to let go is too often assuaging one's own discomfort. It's a bit too guru-like and borders on arrogance to me.

A companion's response to "letting go" mythology

When I am asked about "letting go" dialogue with a non-responsive patient, I encourage loved ones and helpers alike to take a middle ground. We don't know for sure if a coma-like person may be holding on to not disappoint their family by giving up or if they are even willfully holding on at all. Perhaps they would indeed be relieved to feel they no longer have to fight. On the other hand, it may be that their survivalist nature compels them to keep fighting regardless of emotional variables. Perhaps their heart muscle remains strong when everything else has failed. They would love for it to stop beating but it won't. We will never know these things.

What we can always do is consistently convey our love. Then, we may offer our nonjudgmental support for whatever work they may be doing inside themselves. When my dad was dying of liver cancer in 1998, those of us who loved him had the opportunity to convey our love continuously. When he became non-responsive, I told him he had my support if he felt the need to hold on and fight for some reason or if he was tired and wished to rest from the fight. Loved ones always agree with me that it just seems most respectful to cover either direction.

Not understanding a dying person's timing for taking their final breath, I am curious to watch how family members use the time. Observers usually come up with their own theories about the timing of a dying person's last breath. It's not really important to me, though it seems important for loved ones and other companions to speculate about it. I just see it as an opportunity for anyone present to talk more about their relationship with the one dying. Perhaps such an exercise will increase their comfort level with dying. With such dialogue they are already engaged in the work of mourning.

Companioning means having no investment that anyone let go of anything.

Companioning means having no investment that anyone let go of anything. Even if we have our own theories about the nature of attachment, our obligation as companions is to invite others to muse about theirs and honor that there is always more happening than anyone can fathom. We create room for not knowing as well as hypothesizing about the way of things. We prefer the language of reconciliation over the language of letting go.

Chapter 14

"Stages of Dying" Mythology

In 1969, psychiatrist Elisabeth Kübler-Ross wrote a very important book called *On Death And Dying*. It was a reflection of her dedication to increase public awareness of the misunderstood needs of the dying. Many who support the dying today feel a sense of gratitude to Dr. Kübler-Ross for her courage and outspokenness with little or no support for her work during much of her career.

This spirited little physician delineated what she observed as five "stages" of dying: denial, anger, bargaining, depression and acceptance. She has since written and spoken that it was never her intention to suggest the stages be a formula the dying should follow, but of course, many helpers adopted them as such. The more concrete-thinking part of our culture welcomed having the frightening and complex issues of death and dying reduced to a simple prescription to follow. "What a relief that somebody finally gave us the stages," we sighed.

We now realize that while some dying people identify with the Kübler-Ross stages, an equal number do not follow that profile or only partly relate. Her stages of dying are familiar with most of us who work with the dying. We often recognize their presence in some form. We had to start somewhere and the Kübler-Ross "stages" were one of the first user-friendly models offered.

The danger, of course, with "stage" theory is that we confuse what actually does happen with what *should* happen in one's dying experience.

Many moons ago, I was having a conversation with the staff of a local nursing home about these matters. An enthusiastic young helper volunteered that he was currently working with a resident in "stage one" trying to skip "stage two" and already flirting with "stage three." He was trying to convince his patient that she needed to acknowledge her anger or it could be a serious problem with her. Did I have any advice?

I was reminded how concretely some people interpret stages. It's tempting for less flexible thinkers to adopt them as a prescription to follow, like this lad. I invited him to allow his patient to teach him about how she needed to travel to her death. Kübler-Ross's stages can help us identify some of what dying people struggle with. I encouraged him to soften his expectations for the route one takes to death. Each individual defines anew the nuances of dying.

Holding too tightly to what Alan Wolfelt cautions as a "progression of predictable and orderly stages" risks disenfranchising the one-of-kind, irreplaceable quality of each person. If we are too rigid in our expectations, we may unwittingly discount a lifetime's worth of hard-fought-for individuality and integrity. Wouldn't it be sad to judge or minimize one who is dying just because she doesn't conform to some prescriptive "stage model?" Yet it happens.

If we companion dying people long enough, we will inevitably observe some who do parallel the Kübler-Ross stages perfectly. Some will only partially identify with her stages, others not at all. Regardless, as companions we steadfastly validate the importance of each person's unique dying experience as a valuable story continuing to unravel.

Part 5

Reconciliation Needs Of Dying

About the Reconciliation Needs

When I first began working in hospice, I became inspired by how the reconciliation needs Alan Wolfelt articulates in his writing and work with bereaved people beautifully parallel the needs of dying individuals and their families. After all, aren't both groups mourning scores of changes and losses? You bet!

The reconciliation needs of mourning provide the most accurate and usable context for supporting one through dying I have ever found. These are needs that everyone experiencing loss struggles with on some level. I really can think of no exceptions.

When dealing with loss, the concept of *reconciliation* seems much better companioning language than popular grief literature words like *recover* or *resolve*. Working toward reconciliation means honoring that the impact of loss never completely goes away. It means with healing, loss can find its way into a context of meaning that can be lived with and integrated into a healthy new reality.

To *resolve* grief, or *recover* from loss, suggests that grief should be over at some point. I've noticed how these words inadvertently set grieving people up for failure. "What's wrong with me?" I've heard so many ask. "It's been years and I still sometimes hurt inside. I should have *recovered* from that loss by now. What am I not doing right?" Reconciliation is more about making peace with or finding a sense of forgiveness and belonging (mercy) for what is painful versus believing the goal is to make it go away.

Reconciliation Needs Of Dying

1. To acknowledge the *reality* of impending death
2. To tolerate emotional and spiritual pain
3. To acknowledge changing *relationships* to self and others
4. To acknowledge changing *self-identity*
5. To search for *meaning*
6. To create an understanding *support* system

Reconciliation needs of dying are not "stages." They do not represent a formula or prescription to follow. They intermittently surface asking to be reckoned with, then subside. These needs intermingle with each other in differing levels of intensity and duration unique to each person.

Chapter 15

Reconciliation Need 1: To acknowledge the reality of impending death

One sunny afternoon during my college years, I was out watching local motocross racers take their dirt bikes through the paces behind Horsetooth Reservoir in Fort Collins, Colorado. I was standing on the bank with other spectators when a rider came flying up over a dirt mogul heading straight for us with the throttle stuck wide-open.

I remember watching him roar in my direction and thinking, "This guy is gonna turn any second." When it became clear he wasn't, I tried to side-step him but not soon enough. He clobbered me at a pretty high speed, sending me tumbling backward through the air, the bike's spinning rear tire pulling one shoe and sock off my foot.

The impact put me into a state of shock. I was conscious, though I was lying flat on my back feeling nothing. I lowered my eyes and was in full view of my body but had no physical sensations. I was in complete paralysis. People gathered around me asking if I was all right but I could not speak.

I thought, "How curious. Nothing to do but lie here." Thankfully, after a few minutes, sensation began to return at my outermost extremities—my fingertips, then toes, then gradually my feet and arms, and finally feeling came back to my entire body. It was good news and bad news, though. Good news—I was tremendously relieved to know I was not permanently paralyzed. Bad news—I felt like I had been run over by a dirt bike!

I often think of that experience when I'm invited to meet new patients and their families struggling with a newly diagnosed terminal illness. I find them in various states of reality shock. Terminal people and their families are often numbed by the untenable information that a life is coming to a conclusion. Each person regains emotional sensation to a changing reality on her own unique time table. Impending death is at first an illusion that comes and goes like the tide. Most of the time, reality settles in more deeply with a tincture of time combined with increased physical symptoms and candid observations shared by hospice and other care providers.

Denial and reality work

The word *denial* is liberaly tossed about by well-meaning helpers as a favorite description for terminally ill people. While I believe there is such a thing as denial, I don't think true denial occurs nearly as often as helpers like to think. I also notice that denial is a term often used with overtones of judgment. For example, one too frightened to look directly into the fire is often considered either weak, willfully noncompliant or problematic.

I've grown to believe "denial" says more about the *rate of speed at which one moves toward an unwelcome reality*. Some people march right up to reality as if they are ripping open a certified letter. The words of Lily Howard, who was newly diagnosed with inoperable cancer, stick in my mind: "I looked him in the eye and said tell me like it is, doc…how much time do I got?" Lily wanted to know as much as possible as soon as possible. "I've never been one to beat around the bush," she said.

Others only flirt with reality, moving imperceptibly slowly, throwing the metaphorical certified letter in a drawer where it may never be opened or even looked at again. These folks simply won't hear or internalize any information supporting a terminal prognosis—yet. Usually, as bodies weaken and pain increases, the dying and their families find their unwelcome letter has been opened for them by Mother Nature and left everywhere they go, in plain sight, where they are forced to at least glance at it.

I also notice that what may first appear to us as "in denial" may actually be a very conscious honoring of an unwritten tradition not to talk directly about things that are frightening or painful. What we first witness may not always be an involuntary psychic numbing or true denial. They may understand perfectly what's at stake. They're just not talking!

Some family mores hold that it is disrespectful or bad manners to speak openly about highly personal issues such as sexuality, death and dying, finances, spirituality and so on. Some families have hidden or longstanding shame connected to these intimate themes, making reference to them only by using code words or phrases. I often notice how some never openly speak words like "dying" or "death," yet know full well what lies ahead.

Denial or etiquette?

Monique and Bill

Monique was a war bride returning from France with her handsome soldier husband to begin their new life together in the land of the free. Monique and Bill had always honored old school values of chivalry, manners and etiquette. Monique was also highly dependent on Bill. He introduced her to this country in 1945, protecting her from many of the less gracious realities of life.

When Bill was referred to our hospice with end stage lung cancer, I was invited to meet them both. I was informed that Monique, in particular, was experiencing "serious denial." I found that in my first private conversation with Bill, he indicated it was "bad form" to speak directly about his dying, especially around Monique, who was very distressed. He and Monique had been well informed by his physician about his terminal status. Bill told me he had no illusions about his impending death but would not care to talk directly about it. He used code phrases like "make the most of it" and "just take it a day at a time."

Monique taught me that she would be willing to dialogue about caregiving issues but would rather not know the clinical particulars of how Bill's disease was progressing. It was too hard for her. Monique would touch on the subject of Bill's dying by using phrases such as "Bill's needs come first" and "Bill has been so good to me." In companioning her, I found that she responded positively when I validated their impending loss by using her same language or code phrases. I became a safe and welcome visitor in their home for several months.

Bill remained consistent with his commitment to protect Monique until his last breath. His style of death mirrored his philosophy of life.

This couple reminded me how important it is that companions honor the unique style in which each person engages reality work.

A case of true denial

Leo and Tina

On occasion, I've marveled at how both patient and family collaborate in maintaining the illusion that death is not a viable reality, even when the patient's body is visibly shutting down before their very eyes.

Leo was referred to our hospice program by his physician who, along with consulting specialists, had decided that further aggressive treatment would be futile. Reluctantly, Leo and his wife, Tina, agreed. We cared for Leo while he rode a slow rollercoaster downward until he died a year later. During that time, Tina firmly refused counseling support for what was often overwhelming and confusing. She struggled desperately to keep at bay the reality of Leo's dying.

"Why is he getting so weak?" she would say.

"What about physical therapy to build up his strength?"

" He's never going to get back on his feet if he doesn't eat. Why is his appetite so poor?"

Since I was not welcome in this home, my role was to companion our frustrated nursing staff, who struggled to patiently explain over and over how Leo's disease was progressing and he had only a limited lifespan. After months had passed, during which our nurses had responded to numerous home crises and the family had repeatedly declined the suggestion that Leo could be better cared for as an inpatient, Tina finally agreed. Leo was falling, confused, combative, and his pain was cascading out of control.

During Tina and her daughter's brief visits to Leo at our hospice house, they were critical and accusatory about the increased pain medication required to keep Leo comfortable. They protested that his level of consciousness was compromised. They complained that lab work was not ordered. They argued about hospice not utilizing IV fluids to hydrate and nourish Leo.

Repeated reviews of hospice philosophy and normalizing what is expected in the dying process seemed unsatisfactory, so Tina and her daughter were reminded they could always transfer Leo to a hospital ICU to be treated aggressively. Mercifully, they allowed him to remain under our compassionate palliative care.

Though I have free reign to greet and assess families for support at our inpatient house, Tina managed to avoid me altogether. Her daughter turned her back to me and would not speak. I respectfully honored her need for privacy and left her with assurances that I would be happy to respond with support if her needs changed.

Leo died comfortably and without major incident from his family. My follow up bereavement phone messages were not responded to but Tina did call back several days later asking that a piece of equipment be picked up from their home. While on the phone, she described what a shock it was that Leo died.

This case repeatedly challenged our bias about people ultimately needing to "face reality." It became very hard to exercise patience, honoring the difficulty this family had in reckoning with a changing, frightening reality. But one of their gifts to us was teaching us more deeply about how companioning sometimes requires great endurance, reliance on our own support system, and reviewing personal expectations for what another's experience should look like. All gentle, respectful invitations for them to take a step toward a changing reality were refused. It was simply too intolerable for them. Leo's death and his physical absence in their lives was more convincing than our invitations.

Regarding reality work, companions remember to:
1. Honor the rate of speed at which one can move toward a frightening new reality. It is not something to treat.
2. Detach from any goal that one should face reality.
3. Listen for code words or phrases that reference one's understanding of dying. Use the same language when communicating with patients or family members.
4. Share truthful observations about physical, emotional or spiritual changes.
5. Make gentle invitations into exploring reality changes with no expectations for outcome.
6. Be a merciful presence to the dying and family as they are able to get their arms around deeper levels of reality.
Companioning language for validating reality work:

1. "As I listen and watch you, what you're describing doesn't even seem real does it?"
2. "I notice it's sometimes helpful for you to be distracted from the reality of what is so rapidly changing in your life."
3. "I notice the reality of your prognosis seems to visit you in short doses but stays a little longer each time."
4. "One of your challenges right now seems to be finding mercy toward yourself about how hard it is to adjust to the reality of dying."
5. "I notice today you need to talk about what was too frightening during our last visit. What do you notice changing?"

Chapter 16

Reconciliation Need 2: To tolerate the emotional pain associated with dying.

"Priceless ain't free."
— Ken Alstad

This need invites people to be merciful with whatever they find themselves thinking and feeling about their approaching death. It encourages them to allow care for their physical needs as well as emotional and spiritual ones.

To companion one through this rocky territory requires understanding that patients and family members will also need a great deal of support in "normalizing" their unfolding experience. The intensity of new feelings and the pain that accompanies them is frightening. Many wonder if it is bearable. To learn from companions that a wide range of thoughts, questions and feelings, no matter how outrageous, are normal and even to be expected under the circumstances, can be a tremendous relief.

Though dying is inevitable, I've noticed that almost every terminally ill person I companion wondered at some time "Can I actually do this thing?" I also observe that with the introduction of the hospice team, which provides information and support for physical, emotional and spiritual needs, patients usually realize they can indeed accomplish their dying.

Embracing the emotional pain of grief is not easy for anyone under any circumstances. An invitation to do so is contrary to western cultural teaching. People who are dying and people who are not dying alike lack understanding for the important role emotional hurt plays in the process of healing. When the reality of impending death begins to settle in more deeply, grief feelings consistent with saying goodbye to all aspects of this world begin to unravel. Among them, feelings of sadness, anger, helplessness, fearfulness, and confusion visit and revisit in no particular order and for no predictable period of time.

Finding ways of holding the emotional pain that comes with loss of health, independence and unrealized dreams is necessary in order to experience some form of OK-ness with dying. People must literally grieve their way to reconciliation. Companions may find themselves in a choice position to validate the dying in their thoughts and feelings. Our relationship with them must always represent a nonjudgmental environment in which they can be authentic. We can confirm what they are probably already discovering: Rarely are people unafraid of their prognosis. In other words, companions welcome honesty and truthful expressions of pain. We may then gently invite the dying and their families to investigate what kind of things are important to them given the changes they are going through.

It is not unusual for some dying people to have fears of uncontrollable physical pain, while others may not fear the pain so much as they hate the sensation of becoming "foggy-headed" from narcotics. For the latter, it may be much more important to tolerate higher levels of physical pain and remain more mentally aware. This is particularly true with younger parents facing death, who perhaps feel the need to remain clearheaded for their children.

Embracing emotional and physical pain is highly individualized

Shalmar

Shalmar was a young Middle Eastern woman (a butterfly) who came to the U.S. seeking treatment for her cancer. Her husband and two young children accompanied their beautiful wife and mother to the University of Arizona Medical Center, where her cancer was treated but unsuccessfully arrested. This family was referred to our hospice frightened and lost. As her physical pain levels became more intense, Shalmar insisted on maximum consciousness, regulating her own pain medication under the watchful eye of our hospice team.

"The butterfly counts not months but moments...and has enough time."
—Rabindranath Tagore

It was often difficult for her family and our hospice team to observe her in such physical pain, yet her final days were respectfully self-directed. Quality of life for Shalmar was measured by remaining conscious for her children as long as possible. She taught us, paradoxically, that by taking less medication to remain oriented, even though her physical pain increased, the emotional pain of saying goodbye to her family was more tolerable.

Ultimately, Shalmar chose to increase her medication sufficiently to become comfortable. She drifted in and out of consciousness. As I visited one afternoon, she roused and described how when she was asleep, she found herself "walking down a path toward Paradise." Shalmar said it was clear she could either continue to Paradise or turn and walk back to be present to her children one more time. She chose to return to speak with her children.

A few days later, Shalmar completed her walk into Paradise, having tolerated perhaps more physical pain than many would choose for themselves. Her choice allowed her the time she needed to find more reconciliation with leaving her children and saying "goodbye" to this world.

Our greatest gift to Shalmar was honoring her need to control her own path to reconciliation. This to me is an example of tolerating physical pain for the right reason. Tolerating physical pain for the wrong reason is not necessary but unfortunately does happen.

The greatest cause of unnecessary physical pain today has to be lack of education. Dispelling untruths about appropriate narcotic use for pain management can be a wonderful gift to the misinformed. A big problem is lack of advanced pain management for physicians and a public that does not understand the diverse role and timing for hospice involvement. Since the advent of hospice in the early 1980s, no one in America ever need suffer physical pain during end-stage illness. Sadly, it is estimated that only a small percentage of those presently eligible to have their physical, emotional and spiritual needs addressed through hospice are actually receiving it. Referrals are made late, often leaving patients and families to suffer on their own without the comprehensive support of hospice.

Whether or not hospice is involved, there are those who may not have a social or family support system or who choose to isolate themselves from the one they do have. The loners who have simply been very private people sometimes teach us they prefer to tolerate their emotional or spiritual pain with minimal company of others. For them, our most sincere offers of companionship may be declined. We may never be privy to the innermost thoughts and feelings of this population, who have been conditioned to suffer in silence. As companions we may regularly need to find a tolerable place for our own sadness about how some people choose to die emotionally or physically alone.

This is also very difficult for families whose best efforts to invite themselves into their loved one's dying experience are unsuccessful. Our work as companions may include an invitation to family members to express their hurt about how they cannot change what seems to be important to their dying loved one.

Family members must also find ways to tolerate emotional pain

Mrs. Romano

While I am often outspoken about the concept of denial and our invitation as companions to honor it without judgment, I have been referred many times to patients or family members described as being in serious denial—as though I should somehow get them out of it. Mrs. Romano was one such patient, refusing any further aggressive treatment but remaining convinced that her advanced lung disease was always right on the verge of turning around. She consistently demonstrated how it was important to act as though she would soon return to a normal lifestyle though she was diminishing before our very eyes.

It is interesting, however, to be in the presence of dying people who blatantly deny any implications their malady is anything more than flare-up of a familiar chronic condition. I am grateful, though, that our Creator has endowed us with the ability to protect ourselves against the full impact of realities too frightening to withstand, whatever our reasons.

Honor the rate of speed at which one is able to move toward a frightening reality.

Sometimes patients find the courage to soften their protective shield, but often the shield remains up. Our minds are like the Starship Enterprise. "Shields up," barks Captain Kirk. After taking repeated hits from an attacking reality, Chief Engineer Scotty calls back, "Captain, I need more pow'r, she won't take it!" As companions we can only invite those we support (and the key word here is invite) to explore what might be beneath their guardedness. However, companions always *honor the rate of speed at which one is able to move toward a frightening reality*. Mrs. Romano refused all gentle invitations of mine to be curious about her progressive disease, so instead we just reflected on her life and searched for meaning in the simple day-to-day activities she was able to accomplish.

Mrs. Romano's denial was particularly difficult for her adult children, who wanted to talk to their mother honestly about her impending death. They struggled with the dilemma of wanting to honor their mother's discomfort with mortality issues, wishing for a deeper intimacy that often comes with candidly sharing feelings about dying and saying goodbye. Whenever they tested those waters, Mrs. Romano emotionally withdrew from them.

Companioning her children included honoring the different expectations each one had for this experience. We recognized that though they could not be privy to their mother's unexpressed thoughts about dying, they could honor the part of their mother that needed to protect herself against what was too frightening to acknowledge. They could openly convey their love and affection to her and at least express the reality of her dying to each other and to me. "Don't I have wonderful children," Mrs. Romano told me. She did indeed.

I also shared with Mrs. Romano's children a little about companioning philosophy, which seemed helpful to them. We discussed honoring the important role of denial and having mercy toward differing realities and feelings of grief. They began to understand how their own reconciliation needs were unique and different from their mother's. What represented a "good death" for their mother became one which was self-determined, one in which she was honored in the manner she needed to find her way to the end. We spent time exploring ways they could tolerate their own emotional hurt by talking, reframing what they observed from their mother and crediting the importance of saying "goodbye" by showing their love and acceptance.

I assured them that their future bereavement work after such an experience would likely be less complicated because they had practiced an accepting versus confrontational relationship with their mother.

Honoring a dying person's choices and limitations often includes tolerating our own emotional pain for what we bear witness to. It means honoring our own grief while recognizing that each dying person must also engage and reconcile his.

When supporting the dying and their families in emotional pain, remember:

1. This is actually grief facilitation work.
2. Concentrate on joining through active listening, acknowledging the feelings being expressed behind the words. Honor the pain as important, not futile.
3. Model being one who has mercy for their pain and dilemmas. Reinforce permission to hold the feelings as best they can, without judgment.
4. Be sensitive to not backing away, or distracting one who begins to display strong emotions. Resist the urge to offer explanations or advice.
5. Be aware of your personal emotional response to what is happening.
6. Gently invite the dying and their family members to talk about what is painful or frightening about what they are facing.
7. Inquire about other people who may also contribute to their emotional and spiritual support. Assist in connecting them if appropriate.
8. Remain closely connected to your own support system to debrief and nurture your own heart and personal growth.
9. Offer feedback to the one you are companioning about how they seem to feel some relief after embracing their pain in your presence.

Companioning language for supporting the tolerance of emotional pain:

1. "This is new territory for you. You must be feeling many different things."
2. "What are you thinking about and feeling right now?"
3. "These things seem clearly distressful for you. Is it helpful to have people available to be good listeners? Who are those people for you?"
4. "People facing something as big as this are often surprised at the all the feelings that come up. Are you sometimes surprised or alarmed at the depth of feelings you have?"
5. "You seem relieved after our time together. Would you like to meet again?"

Chapter 17

Reconciliation Need 3: To acknowledge and reckon with changing relationships to self and others

"Infirmity can make you a stranger in yer own country."
— Kan Alstad

Companions to the dying and their loved ones understand how part of dying involves an internal process of separating from the world and people in it. When that begins to happen, all relationships a dying person has may undergo some degree of transformation.

Separation is evidenced in sometimes subtle, sometimes dramatic ways. Dying people may lose interest in once intimate relationships with people, things and familiar activities. Conversely, what may have been a distant or lukewarm relationship may become much more intimate as the reality of death becomes imminent. Patients or loved ones may become more needy or dependent. Yet others may appear distracted and begin to withdraw their interest and participation in life as they've always known it. Companions can offer assurance to loved ones that typically, nothing the loved ones did or did not do caused the changes.

Family members who have never companioned anyone through dying often become distressed when their loved one loses interest in eating, talking, reading the paper or watching the news on TV. Not understanding, they often try harder and harder to engage them in activities, conversation and once familiar routines of life. This can be an exasperating dance.

Some who approach the end of life are inspired to strengthen and heal either current or old relationships; others seem not too concerned about making changes in the status quo. Companions are called on to honor what seems to be important in relationship work without strong attachment to outcome. Unreconciled relationships may trigger personal issues with companions. Not surprisingly, our own distress may inspire a sense of urgency to "help" the dying and their families resolve their relationship issues. These are the times when we need good collegial support or professional supervision. As companions, we need to honor the rate of speed at which people struggle through relationship issues, inviting them (and the key word again is inviting) to investigate the status of their relationships if and when it seems appropriate.

Those with limited life remaining may pursue forgiveness in damaged relationships. Others may only find a neutrality or a time of truce from estranged or discordant relationships. Companions are invited to remember that wherever relationships end in the evolution of one's life journey, the aftermath for those remaining can always be worked with. Are there ever complications? Sure, but the leftovers become the life-work, the work of mourning, for those who remain.

I was home on a weekday recently and happened to watch a popular daytime talk show. The familiar show host, walking around the stage with little cue cards and microphone in hand, attempted to reduce an extremely complex relationship issue between an estranged young couple to such oversimplified terms it was laughable. Before our eyes, she coerced them into a pathetically inauthentic reconciliation.

The body language of the couple clearly showed their reluctance to "kiss and make up." With the sheer power of her celebrity and the woo of national TV, the show host did in one hour (minus commercials) what it takes skilled, compassionate therapists months to facilitate *when the participants are willing*. It was one of the worst examples of arrogance and ignorance I have ever seen. The show host did the couple no favors and conveyed a terribly misleading message: that complex relationship and self-identity issues as well as the painstaking work of grief can be reconciled by arm twisting. That was magical thinking at its worst. The show host, however, seemed quite pleased with herself.

I was invited to do a little teaching about these needs to a hospice in Orange County, California. I emphasized the importance of allowing patients and families to teach us about their history, communication style and comfort level in addressing sensitive or painful issues. We talked about the importance of honoring and matching the rate of speed at which patients and families toil with these often complicated matters. Connie was a nurse in our group who, toward the end of the workshop, could no longer sit still listening to my "wimpy" approach. She angrily said, "Look, if I see that a son needs to talk to his mother, for example, I'll tell him to get his butt in there and make it right 'cause you may never get another chance and regret it the rest of your life." She went on to describe how on her watch she was going to do everything in her power to see that relationships get fixed!

"Damn...a bulldog," I thought to myself. We had ourselves a cut-to-the-chase, no-nonsense kind of nurse here. Connie and I agreed that our styles were different, yet I couldn't help but notice how uncomfortable she became when her patients didn't match her picture of "finished business." She just went to work on them until they did. I invited the group to try using this self-check question. "Is what I'm about to say or do meant to make *me* feel better, or does it honor the style and tempo of another's process?" I've never been one to vice-grip people by the ear. That's more a treatment model response—"to drag or pull."

I tend to rely on the tenets of companioning as I invite the dying and their families to consider what may be important with whatever time remains. Then I give them space to meander. It bears repeating, however, that companioning philosophy is based on being OK with every outcome. Remember, what does or doesn't get reconciled is not the measure of *value* in our experiences with the dying. I have watched many well-meaning helpers try to choreograph, manipulate and direct the dying experience of patients and their families. Once in a while the actors follow directions and have a positive outcome, but I wonder how often it is the directors' attempts to assuage their own discomfort. These kinds of helpers live under the illusion that they are more powerful than they really are. They are often frustrated and feel inadequate when they can't control their environment. They're riding a fast train to burnout.

Remember, what does or doesn't get reconciled is not the measure of value in our experiences with the dying.

In his latest book, *Awakening To The Mystery*, Stephen Levine relates a beautiful story of how he observed a young blind man who had been separated from his seeing eye dog in a rainy parking lot. Every time the young man moved toward the dog he stepped on its toe, causing the dog to recoil. Levine sensed his own intervening would only increase the confusion in what the man and the dog were struggling to work out between them. Eventually, the young man dropped to his knees and the dog leapt into his arms "like two young lovers." Companioning takes both guts and wisdom to trust there is value in the struggle versus too quickly intervening. It's actually the opposite of "wimpy."

Clearly there are times when professional intervention is welcomed by the dying and their families with relationship and other issues. When companions feel they are getting in over their heads, it is indeed time to request or refer to additional help.

I'm often called on to facilitate dialogue among family members and their dying loved one when there is discord or they just seem stuck. We painstakingly peel away layers of complaints to unmask deeper hurts longing to be voiced. Often when each member has a chance to say their truth in a safely facilitated counseling setting, intense feelings soften considerably. One of the most common ways I companion is to both model and create OK-ness for differences while emphasizing areas of shared likeness. We remove any blame and acknowledge how each member is probably doing the best they can with what they bring to the barn dance.

I've noticed that fewer death experiences than one might imagine include an ideal reconciliation of remaining complex life issues. What I do notice, however, is that whatever state of "working through" dying people and their families are able to accomplish is a befitting reflection of their unique history and personality.

Every death experience includes relationships in transformation. They are sometimes stable, sometimes tumultuous, sometimes intimate, sometimes distant, sometimes honest, sometimes inauthentic. They are influenced by grief responses and longstanding family history. They can be hard or even impossible to understand by those sharing the relationships. Yet no matter what the relationships look like, companions must treat each one as though it is always in a state of sufficiency, even if it has problems.

Relationships with family members and friends are affected

Family relationships can be complex and confounding under the best of circumstances. Some families facing death would drive the best family therapists to seek counseling. Almost all the professionals I know who companion the dying and their families pursue some kind of supervision or collegial reality checking to preserve clarity in maintaining boundaries and to process our grief.

Companions are not expected to be experienced counselors, unless that's what you already are. But I do think an introduction to family systems theory would be essential for any helper to comprehend multigenerational, cultural and social influences on family dynamics. It is important to understand a dying individual inside the context of her or his own family system. Perhaps most important, an introduction to family systems theory provides insight into our own families, which can help us be clearer about our role as helper.

John Bradshaw's book *Bradshaw On: The Family* is a well-written introduction to family systems theory. Also, Elliott J. Rosen's book *Families Facing Death* beautifully focuses on the family system and how it is affected through terminal illness and death.

Companions will hear from patients and family members how terminal illness separates "true friends" and "committed family" from those they thought were dedicated. Some relationships seem to weather mortality crisis and others do not. Some friends and family surprise and disappoint the dying and each other in ways they didn't expect. Conversely, they often describe how unexpected people come out of the woodwork to provide unanticipated support.

Marriages suffer change as one partner becomes the caregiver to the other. If the dying process is preceded by a long, protracted illness, spouses may reflect on how both physical and emotional intimacy changes. Sexual intimacy may have long ago been replaced by a deepening of mutual loyalty, gratitude and strengthening of friendship. Or intimacy may be lost altogether.

For end-stage disease that includes dementia such as Alzheimer's, loved ones have been mourning the leaving of their partner for years. Relationships change from an interdependent cooperative to one partner needing complete care as though he or she were a child. Caregiver spouses wander exhaustively through every dimension of grief, from anger and resentment to the deep sadness over the many losses consistent with caring for one whose mental status, behavior and body have become unrecognizable.

Relationship changes also mean shifting other roles of responsibility to the caregiving partner. What was once shared by two—financial obligations, legal decisionmaking, domestic issues—now belongs to one.

Adult children who assume caregiver roles also struggle with relationship changes. They often describe to me how hard it is to see one who has always been an independent, wise mentor change both physically and mentally into an infant. Parent-child role reversal is a relationship change.

This population often expresses overwhelming relief at the time of death. Those who have cared for a dementia patient usually agree that the indignity of losing one's mind, personality, and self-care abilities is worse than death itself. My wife, Pamela, much longer a nurse than I a counselor, from the beginning of her career has reflected how there are so many health dilemmas worse than death.

All dying people share a relationship with their disease or degenerative condition.

Companions notice how some seem to view their illness very personally, speaking about their cancer, for example, with great familiarity and knowledge. Others may not refer to their ailment at all or else make distant references using nonspecific labels to describe their health changes. Companions honor the language and comfort level each person conveys with her disease. Each person will teach us about the kind of relationship she has with her infirmity.

Douglas felt embarrassed by the physical disfigurement caused by his lymphoma. He was repulsed by it, always keeping parts of his body covered for visitors. Those who loved and cared for him, too, had to remind themselves that his disfigured body housed the loving and precious man to whom they were all devoted.

Each person will teach us about the kind of relationship they have with their infirmity.

Dolores was more philosophical about her disease and how it affected her. She would describe to me how her emphysema invited her to creatively compensate her activity level due to diminished lung capacity. She related to her illness as a kind of obstacle course through which to negotiate. She held no animosity toward her disease. It was more an unwelcome nuisance on which she wasted little energy being upset. She refused to be victimized by the persistent pathology that slowly led to her death.

As the dying reckon with relationship changes, companions may be the first to model that emotional and spiritual suffering is not something to avoid. We recognize it as a condition that lessens by having mercy shown towards it. Many find it a liberating alternative to practice empathy and forgiveness toward their disease rather than disgust.

And what about all those precious ones who remain confused and angry about relationship changes? As companions, we buckle our seatbelts and remain with the dying in those places. They will show us what the process of finishing *their* lives should look and sound like. The companion promise is that we provide one tangible source of acceptance to blanket their experience. Suffering of the heart contains the possibility for healing at any moment.

Relationship to God, religion, philosophy or spiritual practice

Those with a religious tradition usually find a great deal of comfort from it when dying. For some, formal and informal rites or sacraments reinforce forgiveness and a place in heaven. Prayers for strength and courage to face dying are assuring to patients and families and are often a parting ritual shared with the dying at the end of each visit. Regardless of personal belief traditions, companions are always ready to have the dying and their families teach about what sustains them through frightening times.

Others may have long ago been disconnected from a religious practice and show interest in restoring that relationship, perhaps speaking with a clergy member from their denomination. Every patient admitted to hospice around the country is asked about religious or spiritual needs. Often the hospice chaplain or spiritual counselor is welcomed for a visit to further explore these kinds of questions with patients and family members. These are professionals with backgrounds in theology and usually with clinical pastoral training as well. Hospice chaplains are well prepared to support anyone within the context of their own particular belief tradition. In the absence of religious or spiritual preference, they are compassionate, non-judgmental listeners to the dying and their families.

Over the years, I've been awed by the many ways the dying find reconciliation with death as a benevolent mystery. Most dying people either find consolation from their religion or spiritual philosophy or simply find a way to trust what they don't know. My experience has been that only a small percentage fear what awaits after death. Most of the fear reported to me and my coworkers is centered around, "Will I be in a lot of physical pain?" Hospice, of course, offers assurances that pain management is a priority.

One afternoon I stopped by our hospice inpatient house and met the son of one of our patients, who had arrived earlier from out of town. As David and I got acquainted, I learned that he was a theological seminary professor. He practiced a fundamental belief tradition and had always assumed that people who weren't "saved" died a fearful, distressful death. He was curious about my observations.

I shared with him that after companioning the dying for years, I had learned that the "peace that passes all understanding" seems to find its way in some measure to all dying people with few exceptions, regardless of faith tradition. The language people use to describe reconciling their relationship with God, or to the world or any part of life, sounds different from person to person. However, dying people measure the overall value of their lives based on their adopted beliefs, whatever that may have been. Then they rest the sum total of their essence in the hands of the Great Mystery…and off they go.

Perhaps just as many people who approach dying have no traditional religious leanings as those who do. Many consider themselves spiritual but not religious. These people may be comforted by commitment to humanity, nature, or science, and don't seem overly intimidated by the unknown. Many acknowledge a Creator, a Universal Love or Higher Power. Still others strive for higher consciousness or remain focused on the loving relationships in their life. One certainly does not have to be an expert on world religion or theology to be a respectful companion to the dying and their families. Companions offer the gift of nonjudgmental curiosity, inviting all manner of searchers to reflect on their relationship to whatever they consider sacred or meaningful, regardless of how it may differ from our own.

Respecting philosophical diversity

Sheila

One sunny spring day, I drove down to the lovely community of Green Valley, Arizona to meet a patient who avowed herself as a lifelong atheist. Sheila welcomed me into her home, asking that I use no "spiritual" language or make any overtures to discuss religion. I assured her I had no agenda other than for her to teach me about herself.

Sheila was wary of "counselor types," but this gracious and most pleasant woman gradually became comfortable with me. At her request I played my guitar and sang to her, inspiring dialogue about her love of music and theater. She disclosed that when she was a child, her mother, whom she believed suffered from depression, would often slap her, saying, "I don't know how anyone could love you!" Sheila's childhood wounds were deep and unreconciled. Her mother had passed on to her the deep pain of her own woundedness. Sheila tried to understand, but insisted there could never be such a thing as a benevolent God. She did teach me, over the course of several weeks, that she had found several relationships in her lifetime that represented examples of nonjudgmental love.

Sheila said she clung to that rare part of humanity that transcended self-servingness and loved, expecting nothing in return. She thanked me for holding, with compassion, her intimate story so reluctantly shared. I felt privileged to be part of the chemistry in Sheila's struggle to find meaning in her relationship to the world…to life and approaching death.

As Sheila's respiratory disease worsened, our hospice team responded by adjusting medication and levels of care sufficient to compensate for her physical distress. Eventually, she moved to a nearby care facility where we carefully reported to the staff Sheila's atheistic beliefs and her sincere request that they be honored. Within two days she became non-responsive and died with no more or less visible distress than lung patients typically experience.

A few days later, I was deeply troubled to learn that a well-meaning aide at the care home was overheard proselytizing to Sheila while she lay in a non-responsive state how her "dying would be easier" if she just accepted the helper's beliefs about God. Had she been able to hear, and we presume she could at some internal level, I can only guess Sheila would have felt slapped one more time, feeling judged and unacceptable by one more critical parent with an agenda. In spite of Sheila's own unique efforts to reconcile her relationship to life and death, she was cornered and braced to measure up to the unsolicited belief of one more person. This is not what companioning the dying is all about.

There will always be helpers compelled to change the belief systems of others to match their own. I don't think that will ever change. But I would suggest that as companions, our own spiritual beliefs are meant to stabilize us while we join others in theirs. It's my personal bias that if we were indeed securely grounded in our own philosophical or spiritual beliefs, we wouldn't feel compelled to change others as a way to validate our own. Diversity would be seen more as a welcome teacher and less as an intimidator.

When supporting others in relationship work, companions remember to:

1. Always honor and support within the belief system of those we care for.
2. Establish our role as a nonjudgmental listener who is available to "walk with" rather than lead or follow.
3. Invite others to teach us about their relationships, exploring those that emerge as most important at the moment while remaining nonjudgmental.
4. Normalize and demonstrate mercy for however relationships may change during times of adversity or when someone is dying.
5. Honor whatever state of reconciliation relationships may conclude as being sufficient.

Companioning language for inspiring relationship exploration:

1. "As I listen to you, it sounds like you're noticing how some people are responding to you differently. In what ways do you notice your relationships changing?"
2. "Isn't it interesting how people, even loved ones, have different comfort levels in talking about or being around death and dying? What do you find most helpful and most frustrating in your relationships?"
3. "Our culture doesn't do a very good job about educating people on how to support someone who is dying. Based on what you are discovering, what would you tell the world about relating to one who has only a limited time to live?"
4. "On whom or what do you rely to help sustain you through these hard times?"
5. "Are you hard on yourself at times? Do you ever feel pressure to measure up to expectations of others as you go through this experience?"
6. "Sounds like one of your challenges right now includes trying to find mercy for yourself. meaning patience and forgiveness."
7. "So much is changing in your life right now, it makes sense that how others relate to you and you to them would also be affected in some way."
8. "Can you think of any relationships you would like to see changed? If so, do you have any idea for where might be a helpful place to start?"

Chapter 18

Reconciliation Need 4: To acknowledge and reckon with a changing self-identity

Having spent most of my life at the foot of the Rocky Mountains in Colorado, I had no idea the high deserts of southern Arizona held such beauty. I made this wonderful discovery when I had the privilege of working for a hospice that served Cochise County in southeast Arizona. It wasn't unusual for me to log over 200 miles in a day visiting three or four families on their ranches in remote areas. I was in heaven. It was paradise for a wannabe cowboy hospice counselor in a pickup truck.

One morning I was invited to visit a new patient, an old cowboy on a ranch near Sonoita, Arizona. I was given my favorite kind of map, with instructions that read, "two miles off county road, past the water tank one mile, left at second cattle guard." The nurse, describing an earlier visit, said her car bottomed out several times and she had to wait for cows to clear off the road more than once. My heart started pounding with excitement. "You think I'll need my gun just in case I run into a scrape along the way?"

"No," she said. "Just your counseling skills will do and maybe your guitar."

"Damn," I thought. "Well, OK." It was still one of my favorite scenarios.

Over the next six or seven months I made numerous visits to Ross and his wife, Lola. Ross was indeed a bonafide retired cowboy who managed ranches for nearly 40 years in New Mexico and Arizona. When I met Ross, he had traded in his horse for a garden tractor that he rode from the house to the work shed to putter around on small projects to keep himself busy.

"Hop on," Ross would say and I would sit on the front of his tractor and ride with him to the shop, where we would talk.

In his reminiscing, he sometimes agonized with how hard it was to become more disabled and dependent on others. He said he tried not to look in the mirror because he hardly recognized the gaunt face looking back. As I spent time with Lola, too, she also would remark about how

Ross was not the same man he used to be. While both intellectually understood the cause, they mourned the changes in Ross. "I'm no good to anyone," Ross would say. He measured value by what a man could contribute in physical terms. The man who could never abide those who didn't pull their own weight saw himself becoming what he couldn't tolerate in others.

Companioning Ross and Lola involved mostly listening, but I also inquired about the ways in which Ross was unchanged. He held fast to his value system, which sustained him through his working life. We normalized some of the expected physical and emotional changes they might notice along the way. We honored the Mystery about all that we couldn't predict or ever know. We created permission to protest the changes and to mourn the many "goodbyes" they experienced along the way. Only occasionally would I see a misty eye from this stoic ranch couple, but they weren't about to change much from their lifelong buck-up-under-adversity coping style. Though Ross softened a little before he died, it was important for him to "take it like a man."

Making sense of a changing self identity is part of the emotional, spiritual and psychological work with which all dying people labor. Personality and identity development is, after all, a lifelong process, whether you're dying or not. Those dying just begin to live new questions. "Who am I becoming as I face this disease? What good am I anymore and do I still have anything to offer?"

Personality and identity development is, after all, a lifelong process, whether you're dying or not.

Our self-identities are influenced in part by formal education, culture, family and the school of hard knocks. Our perception of self changes as we acquire a trade or profession, marry, become a parent, and develop personal talents. Most of us picture ourselves accomplishing career goals, anticipating retirement and enjoying more leisure time with family. Those who have children and grandchildren anticipate seeing them grow and discover the wonders of life.

Our self-identities are founded on the belief that we will live a full life. Most of us presume we have open-ended years remaining versus only months or weeks to live. When a person begins to hold the reality of limited days to live, the way she begins to experience herself often changes. Physical changes in weight, stamina and motivation begin. New emotional and spiritual questions are consistent with saying "goodbye" to this world and everything in it.

Lack of cultural empathy

Many American cultural values make it difficult for the dying to embrace self-identity changes. America reinforces so strongly the virtue of self-reliance, independence and pulling your own weight that when our ability to do so is compromised, we often feel ashamed and inadequate. The dying are given the message they are a burden on society. Self-identity can quickly change from feeling like an asset to a liability. If I had a dollar for every patient I've companioned who expressed feelings of uselessness, I could get that new paint job on my truck.

Companions can be sensitive to the dying. who may feel increasingly inadequate in what they are facing. We can first validate their legitimate feelings while also sharing our observations about how society values certain characteristics in its citizens. We can be curious about what effect, if any, those influences may have on them. Being careful not to discount their feelings, we can also invite the dying to teach us about personal strengths that have served them over the years. The dying often find it gratifying in their life review to acknowledge the contributions they have made in their lives on civic, personal and family levels.

Some of those facing the end of life are able to adjust to self-identity changes, while others have great difficulty. Companions don't keep score.

Self-identity uncompromised

Rudy

Since I began companioning the dying in 1992, few have impacted my life more than a young career soldier named Rudy. He was dying of cancer when I first met him. I walked down the hallway of his home to his bedroom, passing photos on the wall of him instructing students in martial arts. The photos documented an impressive physical specimen that in no way resembled the skeletal figure I met in the bedroom. I quickly learned that part of Rudy's self-identity work included mourning the loss of his diminished body and a cancer-forced retirement he fiecerly protested.

I learned from Rudy that his entire identity—his lifetime military persona—had been too casually dismissed by traditional-thinking healthcare providers. They had tried to fit the wrong person into a "we're-the-profes-sionals-who-know-what-a-good-death-looks-like" box. You know the one…where everybody needs to stop fighting, let go with grace and make peace with dying, welcoming the relief it brings.

Rudy was having none of that. According to those who provided his care, Rudy had been "noncompliant, resistant and in denial." As we spent time together, he began to teach me how isolated, abandoned and betrayed he felt. No one understood the depth of loyalty to soldiering he had been try-ing so desperately to convey. Not one person cared to ask him about the oath to never surrender he took when he joined the military. Though Rudy clearly understood the rationale behind discontinuing aggressive treatment, he desperately yearned for someone to metaphorically jump into the fox-hole and fight side-by-side with him to the end.

I learned that companioning Rudy meant allowing him to teach me about how his life goals and self-identity had been so involuntarily changed. He badly needed a comrade who was neither intimidated nor judgmental toward his anger and his need to protest surrender. Rudy was a prisoner of war held captive on two fronts: his disease on one and "good death" expectations on the other. I did my best to be a witness to his expressions of grief. More than anything else, Rudy needed acceptance for his need to maintain a fighting spirit contrary to the well-intended advice he had been receiving.

I had the opportunity to also spend time with Rudy's mother, Gwen, who served as his primary caregiver. I shared with her what Rudy was teaching me. She gradually realized that the deep love she felt for her child, her sol-dier, could most help him by honoring his self-identity, though a part of her wished desperately for him to surrender.

The last day Rudy was alive, Gwen called me to the VA where he was being cared for. When I arrived, his family quietly left the room for a moment. I sat next to Rudy on his bed, where his eyes were glazed and he was breathing in short pants, very close to death. Leaning over him, I asked, "What's going on in there, Rudy?"

Though I never would have admitted it to Rudy, a part of me wondered if he was going to capitulate. Was he going to surrender and go quietly into that dark night?

This remarkable young man tilted his head toward me, made eye contact and in a barely audible voice whispered, "Fight."

Some continued to refer to Rudy as "stubborn" and "in denial." I believed he knew exactly what was at stake but held fast to a code of ethics, to an identity he was passionate about. I felt overwhelmed with admiration, sadness and respect for this soldier who was experiencing his version of a battlefield death.

I think of Rudy often as I encounter others like him along the way. He taught me so well about respecting and honoring human beings while they struggle to both hold onto and also adapt to a changing sense of self.

Shortly after I left Rudy's room, he died. Gwen called me the next day to thank me for my involvement and support. Her sense of reconciliation about her son dying grew when she gave up pressuring him to "let go." Gwen was comforted knowing she had changed from a deserter to an ally for her son.

My eyes filled with tears when she described selecting a headstone for Rudy engraved with the words "Beloved Warrior." I was humbled and deeply touched by those profound words.

When supporting the dying and their loved ones in self-identity work, remember:
1. This work is an evolutionary process with no expectation for resolution.
2. Have compassion for the instability that accompanies changing self-identities.
3. Be openly curious about parts of identity that change for better or worse.
4. Self-identity work is grief work. It is saying goodbye to the world and all in it.
5. Self-identity influences the manner in which one dies. Each person will teach us about what represents dignity and integrity to him.
6. Companions are liberated from having to prevent the distress that accompanies self-identity work.

Companioning language for self-identity exploration:
1. "No doubt you're going through some changes. How do you see yourself changing with all you're going through?"
2. "In what way do you feel like the same person and in what way do you feel different?"

3. "Those characteristics that helped you through difficult times before…what are they and how do they help you now?"
4. "As one who is trying to adjust to many changes in your life, what would you tell others who want to be supportive to you?"
5. "Our society seems to emphasize the importance of pulling your own weight. Are you ever hard on yourself for growing limitations?"
6. "You must be feeling many things about this. Does it help to talk about it?"

Chapter 19

Reconciliation Need 5:
Searching for meaning

"Important comes in two sizes—yours and mine."
— Ken Alstad

"Why did God choose me for this disease?" Dora asked as she stared out the window of her room. I was sitting by this young woman—barely 40 years old—who was dying of AIDS. As she continued to stare into space, I noticed my mind scanning for an immediate list of possible responses. My index included, "Oh, Dora, I don't think God chose you for this disease. It's nobody's fault." Next was, "Perhaps you're a person who has more courage to endure this than others." My silent responses began sounding more absurd: "I don't know, Dora, but maybe this is an opportunity to learn some important things you're supposed to learn." I could see this was going nowhere fast. I was heading for, "It's a bummer Dora…shit happens." Knowing Dora, I thought she would have resonated with that expression, but I was amazed at how quickly my mind ran amok. Our conditioning to make people feel better by offering quick explanations and solutions is deeply rooted. Sometimes it takes great discipline for me to remain silent during moments like that.

As I watched her eyes, I found the good sense to just quietly hold with her the immensity of the question. She was engaged inside herself, searching for a context in which to bear this horrible thing she could not stop. But this important work belonged to her. Eventually, Dora turned and her eyes met mine. So I asked if she had any thoughts about that important question. She said no and went on to teach me about how her religious tradition had been inadequate to provide the answers she was looking for.

Those facing death as well as their loved ones may question familiar philosophical and spiritual values or suddenly revisit dormant religious roots. When I observe the dying painfully struggling for meaning, I am deeply touched and inspired. I often tell them, "This search for meaning is such an important thing you're doing! What a good struggle to be engaged in at a time like this. You can count on me to walk with you!"

The search for meaning seems to be Life's way of drawing Her children more deeply into Herself.

While searching, the dying and their families ask, "How could this be happening now?" Or they despair, "Children are not supposed to die before their parents. Why is this happening?" All human beings are prewired with a hunger for cause and effect answers. Immediately after learning of a limited life prognosis, almost everyone intensifies their search for meaning. Minds work overtime to find a place to hold that terrible and often elusive reality. Companions are patient. We become at least one person who will view unwelcome change with compassion rather than fear and loathing. We encourage the search.

Companions are patient. We encourage the search.

For the dying and their families, feeling permission to ask, search and protest may be just as important as actually finding satisfactory answers. It represents participation in one's own healing. It's empowering. Companioning is not about helping one neatly wrap up complex life and death dilemmas into understandable packages. It is not even about targeting relief, although relief often finds its way to the surface. Companions help hold together the tension between the important search for answers and the likelihood of never having them all.

Those facing death will show us the manner in which they search for meaning. Reflecting on their past histories or sharing fond or difficult memories is an example of engaging in the search. Intertwined through all of the reconciliation needs, the search for meaning is present. Dora's why question was in part a reflection of her continued struggle with the reality of her dilemma.

With those struggling to tolerate the emotional pain in reconciliation need 2, the search for meaning is also alive and well. Referring to her dying husband in the next room, Dottie, herself a hospice patient, tearfully said to me, "I never imagined a broken heart could actually hurt inside your chest. The ache is actually a physical thing. How is it that Dale could have gotten so sick and be dying before me? He's always been the strong one."

Reconciliation need 3, relationship work, is filled with searching for meaning. "Why are many of my closest friends not calling?"many reckoning with dying will ask. "I don't understand how those you think will support you disappear and others whom you barely know reach out."

Remember Rudy, the young soldier who struggled so to maintain his self-identity? He also suffered with a desperate search for meaning. He agonized over why so many healthcare professionals could not understand what represented a honorable soldier's death for him. He wondered if a non-battlefield death could still have dignity.

Earlier we discussed honoring the Mystery—the important role not knowing plays in stimulating the search for meaning. With Dora, I saw my role to first demonstrate acceptance of her not knowing, to honor the Mystery. We mused a short while about those things beyond our understanding. I asked Dora if she would like to meet our hospice chaplain and also explore her questions with one specifically trained in her religious tradition. She thought that might be helpful and seemed encouraged.

In the search for meaning, much of the time people dying aren't really solicitous of our advice. Their existential questions are often rhetorical statements of despair rather than requests for our oversimplified solutions. Though we could never know for sure, I believe that most of the times when I have offered philosophical or spiritual explanations to troubling questions, my words haven't had nearly the impact as when I simply validate how difficult it is to understand these deep Mysteries. At some intuitive level, dying people know it is their job to cultivate meaning for themselves.

Cautiously offering advice in the search for meaning

Because of our propensity for too quickly blabbing our truth, I will always champion the need to first join, listen and trust the importance of existential struggle. Yet, I concede, there are times that our input or advice is welcomed by those we support.

"Tossin' a rope before buildin' a loop don't catch a calf."
— Ken Alstad

Information regarding physical assistance, community resources and practical helping strategies can certainly be helpful. Hospice programs are like encyclopedias of information relative to dying…everything you ever wanted to know about death and dying but were afraid to ask! But in whatever capacity we companion the dying,while we practice mostly nonjudgmental listening, it can also be helpful for the dying and their families to hear from us about what others may have found helpful in similar circumstances. I do suggest a few cautions for companions, however:

1. Qualify that, "While these suggestions may have been helpful for others, they may or may not be for you."
2. Invite each person to take from stories shared about others that which seems to fit—and leave the rest. "Make it your own" in other words. They'll do that anyway, but saying it out loud reinforces how your acceptance of them is not contingent on their taking your advice.
3. Reinforce that there's no right or wrong meaning. Their meaning is the only one that matters.
4. Allow for how differently one may interpret the meaning you intended.

No matter what you and I intend the teaching to be behind our suggestions, each person will process it through his own filters. In fact, it will usually be interpreted differently than we expect. Yet, our input is usually bent to fit their needs, somehow.

Sam and Betsy were fighting like cats and dogs. I learned Sam had been a rather demanding person by nature and the heightened anxiety so familiar to respiratory disease was making him nearly unbearable. Betsy was ready to take a skillet to the side of his head. I had met with them a few times, recognizing how the circumstance prevented each from being able to meet the emotional needs of the other. We identified their strengths and explored strategies for how both could do some preventive things to reduce the anxiety caused mostly by Sam's disease. The two had welcomed my support and their feedback was that what we were doing was helpful. Their arguments were subsequently fewer and less intense.

I arrived one morning for a scheduled visit, pulled an ottoman across from their two recliners, sat down and asked, "Well, how has it been since we last met?"

Sam jumped right in."Greg, something you told me last time has been so helpful. I started thinking about it and realized I've been pretty self-centered about this thing. When you told me that a lot of people were much worse off than I am and to buck up and take it like a man…well, that was so helpful."

I thought to myself *How in the hell could he have remotely gotten that from anything I ever said to either one of them?*

The confusion on my face must have shown because Sam said, "Yep, that's what you told me and you were so right. I've been a real shit to Betsy and some of your hospice staff."

By then I just said to myself *Shut up, Greg. Don't challenge an interpretation that's working for Sam.*

Sam, and so many others like him, extrapolate what they need to hear from what we talk about, but dear readers, I am absolutely sure I never said anything close to what he heard. He reinforced to me how when we offer an explanation or a bit of advice, we can't be invested in how people will hear it or use it.

At times, I think it almost doesn't matter what we say. Each person will hear what they need, when they need to hear it. If the words offered are too painful to hear, they'll filter out any threat to their psychological safety. Call it denial if you wish. That is why I will always err more strongly on the side of good active listening and non-fearful presence than I will on the side of a dispensation of our expert wisdom.

Maslow's hierarchy of needs reminds us that no one will likely be able to search for the deeper meanings in living or dying unless their basic safety needs are first met. In addition to food, shelter and medical care, dying patients so greatly need to feel emotionally safe. That is, of course, what this book is about. Having someone who's not afraid to walk into the fire with them gives the dying and their families courage and increases the odds in their favor for finding meaning in their experience.

When supporting the dying in their search for meaning, remember:
1. Without safety in relationship, facilitating the search for meaning will be difficult.
2. The work of joining through active listening always comes first before offering advice or suggestions, then do so cautiously.
3. In the absence of meaning, be present with no urgency to provide it.
4. Listen for and validate what appears to have been meaningful in the past.
5. It must also be OK with us if the dying can find no meaning in their experience.

Companioning language inviting the search for meaning:
1. "What seems to sustain you during this time?"
2. "How have you found your way through difficult times in your past?"
3. "Do the same spiritual or life-philosophy beliefs that you've always held work for you now?"
4. "How is it for you to deal with all the questions that have no answers?"
5. "Are you ever hard on yourself for not knowing what to do?"

Chapter 20

Reconciliation Need 6: To have an understanding support system available through the dying process.

"A lot of folks would do more prayin' if
they could find a soft spot for their knees."
— Ken Alstad

"Hermit" was a name Joe gave to himself. It described how he preferred his privacy and did not need company. He had a few old buddies he met with daily at the coffee shop the past few years but no family. Joe was referred to our hospice by his doctor, who had discussed his terminal status and increasing care needs with him. While he was appreciative of the extensive services hospice offered, Joe initially declined all help except for the minimum number of nursing visits required.

When he was unable to drive himself to the coffee shop, a friend would occasionally take Joe. As he became weaker and homebound, he required more hours of care per day than our hospice could provide. When death was near, Joe reluctantly agreed to come to our inpatient house. He appreciated the care but did not wish for any unnecessary company. He expressed no need for spiritual support or to explore his life in conversation with a counselor or volunteer. Per his wishes, he died quietly with no fanfare and only the necessary contact provided by our hospice staff regarding his essential care needs.

Dying with dignity has been a topic of increasing interest in recent decades. Kübler-Ross awakened our country to the special needs of the dying in 1969 with *On Death And Dying*. In hospice, we recognize that every dying person deserves to maintain the most fundamental dignities, among them adequate physical care, nutrition, pain management and spiritual/emotional support. However, as companions, we allow each person facing death to teach us about what support means to him.

Support systems usually include two main components: attending to complex physical needs and also caring for the emotional and spiritual dimensions of dying. Sometimes both elements are provided by the same person but often these needs fall to several or even many people.

Caregivers

For Joe, beyond his essential physical care needs, dignity meant privacy. Patients like Joe are probably more rare than those who welcome companioning for themselves and their family members. He was also able to live independently and remain functional without much help up to his last week of life. Each patient will teach us about her emotional and spiritual requirements, but for physical care needs, most will have no choice but to require a caregiver.

Caregivers represent a rapidly growing culture in our country. It is a population that often exists in quiet desperation. Caring for the chronically ill and dying can become an all-consuming way of life. While hospice can provide supplies, medication, nursing care, spiritual and volunteer support on an intermittent basis, it cannot provide the 24-hour care needed by many. Keeping up with adequate physical care needs is a frequent and enormously challenging issue with the dying and their families.

So, when patients tell me, "Don't worry—I have a big family and lots of friends," I never assume that means an adequate support system through the dying process. Sometimes the dying take for granted that family or friends will step up to the plate, put their lives on hold and take over their care. Perhaps they can, but often they cannot. I'm also curious to hear if family and friends are the type not afraid to stand in the fire of emotional and spiritual distress. I find out if they are accepting of tears and bursts of anger alike. Are they the type who can listen more than give advice? Are they respectful and nonjudgmental of current and past life choices? Have they ever cared for a dying person before? As the answers to these question become evident, experienced companions can learn better how to augment meeting the needs of the dying.

Family members often have jobs, live out of state or perhaps are not healthy enough themselves to provide needed care for their loved one. If patients can't afford privately paid care, state aid or nursing home placement may be required—which can be a tricky and complicated system to negotiate. These challenges keep social workers busy in every hospice in

General caregiver statistics

Nearly one out of every four U.S. households (22.4 million households) is involved in caregiving for a person aged 50 or older.

1. The average caregiver is a 46-year-old woman who works full time, has a child still at home and spends 17.9 hours per week taking care of her 77-year-old mother who lives across town.
2. Unpaid family caregivers are the backbone of the healthcare system. In 1997, if they had been paid $8.18 an hour (the average between the minimum wage of $5.50/hour and the average pay of $11.20/hour for a home health aide), it would have cost the country $196 billion more than the annual amount spent on formal home care and nursing home care combined.
3. 87% of terminally ill patients are unable to function independently.
4. Friends and family of the terminally ill are relied upon for most caregiving activities. Only 15% of the terminally ill rely upon paid caregivers, and fewer than 3% receive help from volunteers. Spouses/partners comprise 54% of these primary caregivers, while 29% primary caregivers are adult children caring for their parents or parents-in-law.
5. Family caregivers of the terminally ill are under tremendous pressure, attending to the needs of the patient frequently at the expense of their own needs and health. As a result, family caregivers become the "second order patients." For as the suffering and needs of the patient increases, so does the physical, emotional and financial burden of the caregiver.
6. Physical and emotional well-being: family caregivers of the terminally ill exhibit heightened symptoms of depression, anxiety, psychosomatic symptoms,restriction of roles and activities, strain in relationships and poor physical health.
7. Family distress: Conflicts frequently occur as family members are forced to negotiate caregiving responsibilities, differing opinions regarding treatment, and varying levels of acceptance of the patient„s terminal condition.
8. Financial strain: 25% of caregivers lose their jobs due to their caregiving responsibilities. 1/3 of families of terminally ill patients with health insurance report that they have either lost their homes, gone bankrupt or suffered serious financial losses.
9. Social isolation: Frequently the demands of caregiving require that the family member drop all other activities (work, hobbies, social outings). Friends often find the situation uncomfortable, electing not to visit and thereby isolating the caregiver even further.

Refrences

1. National Alliance for Caregiving and the American Association for Retired Persons (AARP). Family Caregiving in the U.S.:Findings From a National Survey, June 1997.
2. National Alliance for Caregiving & American Association of Retired Persons (NAC/AARP). (1997). Caregiving in the U.S.: Findings from a national study. Washington, DC: Authors.
3. Arno, P.S., Levine, C., & Memmott, M.M. (1999). The economic value of informal caregiving. Health Affairs, 18, 182-188.
4. U.S. Census Bureau. (2001). Updated 1/2/01. Accessed 9/2/01. Current population estimates: http://www.census.gov/population/estimates/nation/intfile2-1.txt. Projections for 2035: http://www.census.gov/population/projections/nation/summary/np-t3-f.pdf.
5 & 6. Emanuel, E., Fairclough, D., Slutsman, J., Alpert, H., Baldwin, D, & Emanuel, L. (1999). Assistance from family members, friends, paid caregivers and volunteers in the care of terminally ill patients. The New England Journal of Medicine, (341). pp. 956-963.
7, 9. Sherman, D. (2001). The reciprocal suffering of caregivers. In Kenneth J. Doka & Joyce Davidson (Eds.). Caregiving and loss: Family needs, professional responses. Washington, D.C.: Hospice Foundation of America.
8. Higginson, I. J. (1998). Introduction: Defining the unit of care: Who are we supporting and how? In E. Bruera, & R. Portenoy (Eds.). Topics in Palliative Care, (Vol 2). New York: Oxford University Press.
10. Levine, C. (2001). Introduction: Nature of caregiving. In Kenneth J. Doka & Joyce Davidson (Eds.). Caregiving and loss: Family needs, professional responses. Washington, D.C.: Hospice Foundation of America.

the country. Solving caregiver needs can be financially, logistically and emotionally exhausting for patients and families.

Having been involved in garnering every kind of support for the dying at one time or another, I've repeatedly observed that there are some individuals whose emotional-spiritual and existential needs are so great they will never be satisfied before they die. Remember the discordant relationship between Janelle and her daughter, Julie, discussed in Chapter 6? Some multigenerational, family wounds are so complex that a whole posse of counselors or clergy could neither sort out nor make a significant difference in the time remaining.

In an understanding support system, I look for those who are clear about their limitations in helping—those who can grieve what they cannot change and advocate where they can. If we are welcome, we can always invite the dying and their family to reflect on whatever might be important to them. We can be curious about what would be the best use of the time they have left. But remember, we cannot hold the expectation that all life dilemmas must be resolved before death.

One of the most poignant scenes for me in the movie Forrest Gump was when Forrest's friend Jenny came back to spend time with him at the old homestead. The two are walking the property and Jenny suddenly realizes they are in front of the little house where she grew up as an abused child, always praying to fly far, far away. She suddenly is overcome with pain and begins throwing rocks at the house, breaking windows, finally collapsing to the ground, sobbing. Forrest approaches her slowly, kneeling down near her as she sobs, and beautifully reflects, "I guess sometimes there just aren't enough rocks."

"I guess sometimes there just aren't enough rocks."

The fact is that many people take with them to their death unreconciled issues. So, whatever gets healed we celebrate and that which doesn't we honor as their best attempt with what resources they had available. I emphasize again that death experiences that leave loose ends or unresolved dilemmas must be just as valued as any other. Plus, any complications left over with bereaved family can always be worked with!

I encourage companions to see ourselves as compassionate teachers for other potential supporters who may not understand companioning philosophy. For the sake of the dying, please don't hesitate to be outspoken with your companioning wisdom.

Occasionally, honoring another's right to choose the manner in which to die and still be a responsible friend or companion is a sticky wicket. It is especially difficult if the dying one becomes physically or mentally unable to care for himself and refuses essential help. Perhaps he cannot take medications correctly or has had several serious falls due to increased weakness.

In addition to hospice, most communities have Adult Protective Services or a local Council on Aging that can offer guidance and even intervention regarding safety issues, if needed. They at least can make an assessment and advocate for additional services if there exists a possible danger to self or others.

In hospice we occasionally make those kinds of referrals if a patient living independently can no longer care for herself or appears to be neglected. With the moral dilemmas of possible neglect, abuse or diminished capacity to make safe decisions, companions should not have to feel burdened to know what to do. When in doubt, contact local social services for assessment and guidance.

When assessing the dying for adequate support, remember:
1. If hospice is not involved, contact your local hospice. **Anyone can make a hospice referral**. Tell them about your friend; they'll know what to do.
2. Invite the dying person to teach you about what represents the best kind of support for him. He is the expert about his own quality of life needs.
3. Within your ability, investigate other possible community resources that may also provide services.
4. Companioning the dying and their families has its limitations. Regardless of how extensive one's needs are, end of life doesn't have to be an emergency.
5. Good support means honoring what gets reconciled and having mercy for what doesn't. "Sometimes there just aren't enough rocks."
6. Companions are always respectful teachers for other helpers in passing on companioning philosophy.

Helpful language when inquiring about support needs:
1. "Tell me about your support system."
2. "Does your support feel nonjudgmental and respectful of your lifestyle?"
3. "Are you a person that likes company or do you more prefer your privacy?"

4. "When people do spend time with you, what do you find most helpful from them?"
5. "Would it be helpful for me to check out other sources of support for you for some of the concerns you've expressed?"
6. "Is it hard to let others reach out to you?"
7. "Would it be helpful to talk about ways you could ask for what you need from the people in your life?"

Part 5

Companioning Children

Chapter 21

Companioning children when someone they love is dying

The Tender Elf

The greatest poem
ever known
Is one all poets have
outgrown:
The poetry, innate,
untold
Of being only four
years old.

Still young enough to
be a part
Of Natures great
impulsive heart,
Born comrade of bird,
beast and tree
And unselfconscious
as the bee--

And yet with lovely
reason skilled
Each day new para-
dise to build
Elate explorer of each
sense,
Without dismay, with-
out pretense!

In your unstained
transparent eyes
There is no con-
science, no surprise:
Lifes queer conun-
drums you accept,
Your strange Divinity
still kept...

And Life, that sets all
things in rhyme,
May make you poet,
too, in time--
But there were days,
O tender elf,
When you were
Poetry itself!

Christopher Morely

Christopher Morley, in his beautiful poem, gives us a sense of how vulnerable and yet resilient children are. Because every child is unique, his or her response to one who is dying will be different, but all share some special needs at such a time. If we can be prepared to nurture their needs with patience and a bit of wisdom, children will more likely experience the death of a loved one with fewer complications.

Those of you who have companioned a child through an experience with dying no doubt have been inspired by their divine capacity to reconcile life's queer conundrums. Let's review some of their special needs during such a time, and ways to meet them.

Children grieve but also need to mourn in anticipation of loss

Children, like adults, first encounter the need to mourn with the knowledge someone they love is dying. "For a flower to grow," writes Alan Wolfelt, making an analogy to children, "the plant must receive adequate nutrients from the soil, adequate water and sufficient sun. It also needs protection from pests, disease and invasive weeds. The gardener who understands and helps his plants meet these needs will be rewarded with a lush, healthy garden."

We remember that *grieving* might be described as all our internal thoughts and feelings relative to loss, while *mourning* describes the outward expression of grief. Though crying, sharing memories and participating in funeral rituals are familiar examples, other expressions of mourning may be represented in the form of play, creative artwork or music. Mourning can also be looking at photos, polishing an old car or any activity that would convey outwardly one's feelings of grief. The more we understand how children mourn in anticipation of a loss, the more likely we will earn and maintain their trust.

Children need to play

As his dad became sicker at home with cancer, 11-year-old Miguel asked me about what the hospice inpatient house was like. He wondered if there were areas to skateboard and if the TV in his dad's room would have connections for his Nintendo game. Conversely, adults will usually ask about things like visiting hours, if they can spend the night at the bedside and is there counseling available for themselves and family.

Walking with children through loss requires understanding about the important developmental truth that **play is the work of children**. Because children continue to engage in play, it may appear as though they are not affected by a loved one dying. Not true. Behaving like a child is their assignment. It doesn't mean they're not struggling internally to accommodate a confusing new reality. It doesn't mean they don't have questions or that they're not afraid or sad. The timing and manner of speaking up or acting out is unique to each one. Young Miguel was scouting out play conditions he knew would help him cope.

Many children are just beginning to understand and develop respect for sacred and profound events. They have short attention spans. They're silly and playful. They are louder than adults (usually) and quick to remind us almost everything except play is "boring." Certainly they need supervision and coaching to learn appropriate behavior around new experiences, but it's helpful to remember a child's only job is to flourish in a manner consistent with her age. Thus, supporting children through a loss requires an extra measure of patience. It would be unfair to hold children to the same behavioral standards as we would adults.

We can be assured that some form of age-appropriate play will be the medium children will use to process change. It's a genetic endowment they adeptly use to help mitigate frightening, painful or even joyful experiences.

As well-informed companions to children, we can become better prepared and teach others who may have unrealistic expectations about how children should cope when trying to accommodate the reality that someone they love is dying.

Let's go over some principles that will help us.

Principles for companioning children

Principle 1: Tell the truth

Just like bats, children have excellent built-in radar systems. Long before adults realize it, young and older children alike tune in and respond to changes in their families due to the illness of a member. Children need perceptive adults to watch for and validate the child's observations about changes around them when a loved one is dying. Children need confirmation for what their radar is telling them.

Children of any age who show an interest or ask questions about a loved one who is dying deserve to be told the truth. Children *can* tolerate the truth. Children *want* to know the truth. Children *need* to know the truth so they can respond to an authentic reality versus a fabricated, misleading reality.

We already know children intuit the truth long before adults around them ever suspect. They read body language and feel the tension. They overhear conversations about the person who is ill and take their cues from adults about how to respond. If there is secrecy or incongruence practiced by their role models, children may assume that whatever is happening is too horrifying to be talked about, or that they are somehow the cause.

Lynn, a young mother, shared with me how when her father was dying, her family was sitting at the dinner table one evening when a wave of grief overwhelmed her. She was trying hard not to become emotional when her five-year-old daughter, Amanda, asked, "Mommy, are you mad at me?" Lynn let her daughter know that she was just sad about grandpa dying. She expressed amazement later to me at how perceptive Amanda was, yet how easily she could misinterpret what she witnessed. Lynn also recognized that her pretense of equanimity was no match for Amanda's radar.

On Magical Thinking

When you are supporting children who love someone dying, misinformation or half-truths about the details of death and dying is not helpful.

Correct information can help children avoid catastrophic magical thinking about what s happening around them. It allows them to more accurately contextualize behaviors they observe and conversation they overhear.

Eleven-year-old Sam noticed his dad becoming increasingly withdrawn and his mother often tearful. He imagined they no longer loved each other and were heading for a divorce, like his friend Adam s parents. He also thought he was somehow the cause because of the expensive new braces on his teeth. Sam often heard his parents discuss financial difficulties. When he was finally able to give a clue about his fears, Sam s parents were surprised but happy to assure him they loved each other and were not getting a divorce. They were able to openly acknowledge their feelings of deep sadness that Aunt Peggy, his dad s sister, had cancer and was probably going to die. And further, half the cost of his braces was covered by insurance. Sam was so relieved.

He said he already knew Aunt Peggy was dying from talking to his cousins. He, too, was sad but had never doubted his family could find their way through Aunt Peggy s dying together.

If youngsters begin creating an assumptive view of an experience around false information, imagine how confusing it is for them to readjust their thinking and feelings when the truth finally catches up with them. It fosters a mistrust in adults and, worst of all in my opinion, a doubt of their own intuitive judgment. *Children are magical thinkers, and explanations they can conjure can be much more harmful than the truth.*

Principle 2:
"Dose" out information using age-appropriate language

Helping children reckon with the reality of an impending death loss means thinking beforehand about how to respond to their questions when asked. It means not overwhelming them with too much too soon, or conversely, withholding facts that could be meaningful and help them adjust.

Short, simple and honest is a good rule. It's most helpful to use language consistent with their developmental age and measure it out in doses to match their attention spans. Short, simple and honest is a good rule. If we're not sure what they may want to know, we can always ask them if they want to know more about their loved one.

How do you know how much to say?

"I don't think Rachel understands her mother is dying…at what point should we tell her?" asks a parent or adult family member. I invite parents and caring family members to first ask themselves these kinds of questions:

1. Is Rachael showing curiosity about dying or death?
2. Does my gut tell me I'm being unfair, at this time, to withhold the truth?
3. Am I protecting her from information that could prevent her from a more intimate goodbye?
4. If she knew the truth, could she do or say things now that could have future importance to her as she looks back on this time?
5. Am I afraid the truth might might harm her in some way?
6. Do I know a wise or more experienced person to use as a sounding board?

Every family has its own comfort level with conversation about dying. But I've noticed that usually after investigating these questions and finding some qualified supporters, parents usually feel better about how much to disclose to their children. Still, each family needs to determine the appropriate timing and manner of doing so.

Children have taught me to be prepared for direct questions. They often cut right to the chase. Seven-year-old Rachel will look straight at you and ask, "Is my mommy going to die?" We better be ready for that one. Companions can help parents and other adult family members prepare beforehand for such pointed questions with honest and age-appropriate language.

"What an important question, Rachel!" I'll sometimes answer when asked. "Your mommy is getting sicker and is probably going to die fairly soon, though no one knows exactly when. The doctor thinks maybe in one or two days."

Family members can offer assurances to Rachel that she will always be loved and taken care of. They can hold her when she cries and reinforce that what's happening is not her fault. Being truthful with that piece of information allows for the possibility of children saying "goodbye" in whatever way they need to. Rachel can ask questions of her mother and others she may not have asked otherwise. I offer these suggestions regarding how much to disclose and when:

1. Reality check your question with qualified helpers such as a hospice bereavement counselor, social worker, chaplain or school counselor.
2. Use the help of these support people for age-appropriate language.
3. Allow them to be with you when talking to your children, if that would feel helpful.
4. Remember that children can handle the truth when supported with love and understanding.
5. Having done your homework, trust your own intuition on these matters in spite of what others suggest. (Remember…no decision we make as parents is 100 percent right or wrong. We just try to increase the odds in favor of a healthy experience.)

Principle 3: Allow for tides of pain to flow in and out

A child's aching heart is one of the hardest things to be in the presence of. Yet, understanding and honoring the need for their small hearts to grieve, to legitimately mourn, is essential for their healing to occur. For us to tolerate this distressful truth, our brain really needs to be strong because our heart would tend to over-rescue every time.

Children want and need to express their feelings. As companions, we need to wrestle with the importance of not squelching a child's expression of tears and authentic hurt.

The manner in which we use hugs and gestures of comfort and the intensity with which we physically hold or touch an emotional child needs to convey a supportive presence, not a "stop what you're doing" kind of energy. It's often during these moments when we as adults could perhaps use some comforting for what we cannot fix. "There, there, it's OK…don't cry everything will be OK," may risk stopping a child from healthy and necessary anticipatory grief. All of us can pay closer attention to whom those messages are intended.

Companions need reminding that children come prewired with a protective switch that helps regulate the amount of emotional pain they can tolerate.

Companions need reminding that children come prewired with a protective switch that helps regulate the amount of emotional pain they can tolerate. It's really a very cool thing to watch! We've all seen the way children turn their attention on and off. Rachel can ask, "Is my mommy going to die?" and in the middle of dad's response, interrupt with "Can we have corn for dinner tonight?" while heading outside to play. I find it both fascinating and relieving to watch children toggle the switch on and off.

Like us, children need to find ways to tolerate their emotional pain while someone walks with them through it. They need loving adults who can allow them their sadness without an urgency to fix it. Companions must have faith in the paradoxical but critically important role *hurt* plays in *healing*. "Rachel, you seem sad today. Are you thinking about your mommy? I thought so. I'm feeling sad about her, too. Sometimes we just need to cry, or talk about our sadness, don't we? Could you use a hug?"

To help bring comfort to children in their hurt and fears, I recommend a wonderful children's book called *The Invisible String*, by Patrice Karst. It beautifully teaches how we are all attached to each other by an invisible string made of love, regardless of our life circumstances. It reinforces how love transcends time and space, life and death, keeping us connected.

Principle 4: Give children options for involvement

Depending on the nature of the relationship a child has with one dying, he will teach us about his comfort level in how much or little he wants to be involved in direct care or contact. Children cope better (and have less complicated grief) when offered the opportunity to have free access to a dying loved one and to contribute something of themselves to the experience.

For younger children, gifting the dying with their artwork or occasionally serving as a "gopher" (go-for this, go-for that) can be very meaningful. Children should never be coerced to participate over their objections, but neither should they be intentionally left out of opportunities to feel a part of caring for a loved one who is dying.

Some kids may choose not to visit but may be curious about the reports of others who do. This may be more true with pre-adolescents and teenagers. It is important, however, that youngsters be kept informed about how their dying loved one is doing and be continually given the option to visit. They often change their minds. Whatever they choose, however, adult companions need to honor their choices without judgment or blame.

I keep a tub of art supplies handy for work with children. One of my best discoveries has been colorful plastic beads , some of which have letters on them. Using elastic string and barrel catches found at craft stores, children can make necklaces or bracelets for their loved one with messages spelled out. I have participated with many families where the one dying was wearing a colorful beaded necklace bearing the message I—L-o-v-e—Y-o-u, made from the hands of a tender elf. Children are gratified when their gift of love is received, whatever it is.

Principle 5: Children need constant assurances of love and safety

Young children sometimes become more clingy, whiney or easily frustrated when there is change in their family. Parents may notice regressive behaviors such as thumb-sucking, baby talk or bed wetting. Older kids may become moody or quiet. Adult companions can be prepared for these changes and offer an extra measure of patience, affection and assurance.

Under the best of circumstances, adolescence is difficult. It makes sense that when one they love is dying, teens may act out or even become super responsible, perhaps trying to parent younger siblings as their way of protesting how life is being unfair. Adult companions need to be especially patient and non-shaming with these behaviors. Adolescents often see themselves as the center of the universe and may be unable to empathize with the effects of impending loss on themselves or others.

It may be helpful to review with children who is available to respond to their needs if they need extra support at school, church, friends' houses or community activities. When leaving the house, parents can make sure children know when they will return and how they can be reached. Those who support children can read more books out loud, participate in more play and maintain family activities.

When her mother was dying, fifteen-year-old Heather decided to stay out all night. Her panic-stricken family located her the next day at a friend's house, but not before spending an agonizing night searching and calling all known acquaintances. Heather was angry, hurt and protesting the many aspects of not having an active mother in her life.

If teen behavior ever seems destructive or extreme, professional help may be needed. Caring adults can be watchful for patterns that do not gradually return to normal levels of functioning over time. Relative to bereaved adolescents, (and those experiencing anticipatory grief), author and child psychologist Dr. Alan Wolfelt suggests adults watch for extended symptoms of:

• Chronic depression, sleep difficulties, restlessness and low self-esteem
• Academic failure or indifference to school-related activities
• Deterioration of relationships with family and friends
• Risk-taking behaviors such as drug and alcohol abuse, fighting or sexual acting out
• Denying pain while at the same time acting overly mature

It can be helpful for all children to hear about the ways we as adults take care of ourselves when we are sad or scared.

It can be helpful for all children to hear about the ways we as adults take care of ourselves when we are sad or scared. We can talk openly about the things we do to support ourselves and then invite kids to teach us about what works best for them.

Principle 6: Honor the Mystery with children

Relative to the many unanswerable questions about life, death and illness, it is always important to be truthful about what we don't know. Companions can assure children that all of us wonder about things that have no answers, yet we can still be curious about what explanations they may have for those difficult questions.

Trying to better understand the Mystery surrounding dying, disease, health and spirituality is a lifelong pursuit for all of us. As adults we may share our own personal spiritual and philosophical explanations, but I'm also a proponent of honoring how there are many theories about these complicated areas of life. Always asking children what they think teaches us about their perceptions and provides an opportunity to address misunderstandings and validate feelings.

Principle 7: Encourage growth-enhancing activity...kid's stuff

During the year Katie's mother was dying, Katie remained involved with her soccer team, playing several invitational tournaments as well as her regular season schedule. Her coach was sensitive to the difficulties in her personal life and invited Katie to participate in some of his own family activities. Katie's grandmother, who was raising Katie and her sister, expressed gratitude that her coach and family helped provide stability for Katie this way.

Like tender young plants, children are drawn toward the sun and light. Life and all Her awaiting discoveries call out to them. Christopher Morley's poem about the tender elf reminds us how children are spontaneous, curious and needy of exploring new things. They are doers more than dialoguers. They are people of action. Embracing whatever tomorrow holds is part of their hardwiring. Growth-enhancing activities can be a welcome relief from processing the powerful emotions consistent with loving one who is dying.

Adult companions can help children anticipating a loss by softening expectations a bit for school work and having

A Blessing
May we all remember that children enter the world with: unstained transparent eyes, no conscience, no surprise: Life s queer conundrum they accept, their strange Divinity still kept.
May we trust in their capacity to cope and heal when surrounded by love and healthy role-modeling.
May we celebrate their differentness, laugh at ourselves and cultivate a forgiving spirit, knowing for certain, Life sets all things in rhy m e
Finally, may we always look for Life s poetry and Gra c e even when we sometimes feel lost and our hearts are aching.

patience with mood changes and horseplay. Other ways to companion children might include encouraging their involvement in sports, art, dance, music and other expressive activities. Or as Miguel taught us earlier, finding a place to hook up a Nintendo at the hospice house.

We can encourage peer relationships and outings with their own or other families, such as Katie with her soccer family. Most of the time, however, we as adults won't have to make the suggestion. Kids will be bugging us about what they want to do. We can, however, do our best to create schedules that allow for their growth-enhancing activity.

Principle 8: Look for an opportunity for a positive, life-changing experience

Nobody volunteers for terminal illness to show up in our lives. Yet, the fact remains that companioning a loved one through dying can represent a healthy precedent for children.

Think about it for a moment. How else are children going to learn how to cope with sadness, unknowns and the grief of anticipated loss if they don't have good role models and opportunity to practice? Though it's not the kind of practice we go looking for, as parents or loving companions we can facilitate a positive experience with lifelong implications, as long as we recognize the opportunity before us.

If children are exposed to death in a way that makes it approachable and safe to express tears and laughter alike…if they have adults sensitive to companioning principles, the rest of their lives they will more likely find death experiences less daunting.

Though this logic usually appeals to moms and dads who want the best for children, they sometimes need helpers who can teach and model the principles of companioning for them. We all have the ability to become one. Cool, huh?

Summary and encouragement

• Children need to mourn in anticipation of a loss. They need to express outwardly what they feel inwardly. They can best teach us about their unique way of anticipatory mourning when we are accepting and non-judgmental.

- Children will cope in a manner consistent with their age group. Coping is apt to look silly and playful at times. Adults need to recognize how children mourn differently from adults and from each other.
- Play is the work of children. Adult companions need to support children's play for the way it helps them process information and reckon with the challenges of loving one who is dying.

Chapter 22

Final Thoughts

When death comes and whispers to me,
"Thy days are ended,"
let me say to him, "I have lived in love
and not mere time."
He will ask, "Will thy songs remain?"
I shall say, "I know not, but this I know:
that often when I sang, I found my eternity."

— "Fireflies" Rabindranath Tagore

My dad was fond of saying, "I couldn't carry a tune if it had handles," yet he sang his songs nevertheless. Sometimes he actually sang little ditties or choruses from the classics. But if singing has to do with giving expression to the music inside us, then I guess he metaphorically sang by living his life with gusto and curiosity. In his retirement, this silver-haired former church builder and minister sang by riding his motorcycle all over the country, visiting with strangers along the way. Pop loved meeting new people. Everyone was his friend. He had a youthful wonder and amazement about all the fascinating things in the world. Along the highways, when a sign said "Point of interest ahead," Dad was the guy pulled over reading the plaque then staring out into space, imagination spinning. Maybe you saw him. I miss my dad and strive to be like him that way.

If you and I have the opportunity to invite the dying to teach us about how they sang during their lifetimes, that's a wonderful thing. But we had better buckle our seatbelts, hang on and be prepared to travel anywhere. And the beauty of companioning is that just as many gifts await us as they do those telling their stories.

A few more courtesies and considerations

Companions can remind families of dying persons:

1. Remember that we never know for sure how much the dying hear in their non-responsive state. Assume they can perceive everything around

them at some level, even though they may not be able to give a verbal or physical response. Try not to talk about a dying person in her presence as though she were already gone.

Non-responsive dying patients sometimes arouse and startle those around them by saying, "Please don't talk about me like I'm already dead!"

2. Keep conveying words of love and support. Engage in conversation around the bedside that your family would usually enjoy. Make room for humor as well as tears.

3. Maintain appropriate affection and touch consistent with what your relationship has always been with the one dying.

4. Use common sense about keeping the environment tranquil without harsh noise or annoying bright lights. Some patients enjoy soft music. Ask patients when they are alert about their interest in music, visitors or room light and noise. They will teach you about their preferences. Patients with breathing difficulties often prefer cooler temperatures and moving air (as with a fan blowing nearby).

5. Always tell your loved one when you are leaving and when you'll return, particularly if the one dying is in a non-responsive state. It seems apparent that dying people often adjust the timing of their last breath to correspond with people either being present or not present. Patients clearly may hold on for absent loved ones to arrive and die moments after. They may hold on for particular dates that are important to them, such as anniversaries or birthdays.

On the other hand, families may be vigilant around the bedside for days then leave for a moment to fill their coffee cups and the patient dies while everyone is out of the room. For some, dying is a very private matter.

In an earlier chapter I made reference to Bill and Monique. Here's the conclusion. I was paged very early one morning by Brad, our hospice nurse on call. I arrived at Bill's home to learn he had been non-responsive all night, with his very anxious wife, Monique, and daughter, Carla, at his bedside.

We all sat together, Brad and I offering support and companionship. Monique was up and down, full of nervous energy, feeling lost. I finally said, "Monique, let's go to the kitchen and make some coffee." While we were in the kitchen, this is what Brad witnessed at the bedside.

Understand first that Bill and daughter Carla had historically seen themselves as needing to be strong for a more fragile Monique. The moment Monique and I left to make coffee, Carla leaned over to Bill and said," Dad, Mom just left the room. If you want to go, now would be a good time." Bill took one more breath and died.

As Monique and I were making coffee, we heard from the bedroom, "Mom, you might want to come in here". Monique rushed back of course to find Bill had died. With his daughter as an ally, Bill apparently hoped to spare Monique from what he thought would be an unbearable moment. That would have been completely consistent with his and Monique's relationship.

6. It is just as important to emphasize that the moment of one's last breath may have no observable correlation to anything in particular! This is just as often the case as those deaths whose timing correlates to something specific.

7. When many people are present attending a death, companions can be watchful for some family members who may want or need more "alone" time with the one dying. In particular, spouses may secretly feel their intimate private time is intruded upon by well-wishers and other family members, even though they appreciate the gesture.

Companions can remind visitors to lean on the side of shorter visits than longer and for family members to inquire with each other about the need for personal alone time with their dying loved one.

For patients, being engaged with visitors takes a lot of their energy, which may be in very short supply. As a companion, if you notice energy levels fading, consider inviting visitors to leave if they don't sense the need to do so, unless of course the patient insists they stay.

8. Be aware that with the introduction or increase in medications for pain or anxiety, dying patients may become less conscious. Usually the hospice personnel will prepare the family accordingly but as a non-hospice companion, if you learn medications are soon to be increased that

might render the dying one less responsive and you are aware that some loved ones may not understand the possibility of these consciousness changes, speak up. Family members deserve to know this so they may convey one last time important messages of love or goodbyes.

9. People generally die in the same manner in which they have lived. Personality, values and lifestyle typically remain consistent through the dying process.

Fiercely independent people who protest losing control of their lives may exasperate their care providers by not letting them do their job. Obsequious, compliant people make the most cooperative patients and usually leave this world much more graciously.

Those who historically have been non-expressive with thoughts and feelings will most likely give us less of a clue about their internal experience of dying. But expressive, articulate individuals can give us a play-by-play description of their dying as long as they are conscious.

The eternal optimist will be looking for the silver lining as they approach death. Negative personality types who have always seen themselves as a victims will be bracing for the next catastrophe and perhaps be very needy or fearful to the end.

Caretakers or nurturing types who are dying often remain concerned about how their helpers are coping and whether their families doing OK. But regardless of personality type, some show up to the experience of dying already reconciled to all their life issues. Many are able to satisfactorily work out reconciliation and healing from their fears, old wounds or estranged relationships. Others leave this world with varying degrees of distress and unreconciled pieces of their lives in spite of the all the support available to them. Sometimes there just aren't enough rocks.

10. Some patients want to die as desperately as others want to live. "I don't know what's taking this so long. I just want this to be over" is a familiar reflection of many who endure long (and sometimes brief) illnesses. Delayed gratification is not only a difficult developmental task for children, it's an enormous challenge for many dying people as well. Life continues to invite us to reckon with how we can't always have what we want when we want it. Companions have the opportunity to observe and validate for dying people how trying the experience is on their

patience. We can at least help them feel joined while they conclude what rests solely only their shoulders to finish.

In my experience what seems most effective at times like these is to rely on active listening, "Old Reliable." Usually, this is not the time for guesswork or sharing theories about why dying is taking so long. It's not the time for much talk. The gift of reverent presence seems most respectful.

11. As dying people begin separating from this world, they sometimes refer to seeing people or beings we cannot see. They may tell us about visitations from deceased loved ones, angels or entities unknown. These experiences can be comforting to the dying and inspiring to those of us who companion them. There are many theories about the role these visitations play.

I've been with patients who were clear about who was visiting them and others who didn't know their celestial companions. Mr. Davis described seeing an angel sitting on his sofa. "Did you see her wings move?" he would ask. He also was visited by two little children whom he did not know. He told them, "We're going a-traveling." Others may ask who that is with you when there's no one else in the room. Patients sometimes stare with a smile, reach out or point to something or someone we cannot see.

Companions have the opportunity to be curious with the dying one about who those people are or what those experiences mean to them. It seems most respectful to me to withhold our personal explanations or guesses about them but defer to the wisdom and curiosity of the dying people we companion. Actively listen, ask a few questions but resist the urge to give explanations about "spirit guides coming to show you the way" or "go-to-the-light" kinds of prescriptive instructions. Truth is, none of us knows the meaning of those special experiences. We're only guessing. I can no more explain those special encounters to the dying than I can tell you what your dreams should mean to you.

It seems probable to me that helpers who are quick to give their explanations for these visitations are attempting to comfort themselves as much as help the dying. Perhaps there's no harm done, but I personally would err on the side of trusting the dying to find their own meaning, whether they're able to verbalize it or not. No one has ever failed to find their way out of this world because they didn't get a satisfactory explanation from a well-intended bystander. Curiosity, love, humor and nonjudgmental acceptance are the most important gifts we may offer the dying when bearing witness to these special kinds of experiences.

More lessons learned

Sometimes, out of all the meaningful aspects of companioning, the most important is our willingness to remain open hearted in the presence of one who is experiencing suffering of any kind. Therein lies life's gift of deeper awareness, learning and gratitude for the taking. Compared to all the potential distresses for the dying and their families, a far greater tragedy would be if those of us who have the rare privilege to companion them would sleepwalk past the priceless treasures with our names on them.

The worst thing is not the sorrow or the loss or the heartbreak. Worse is to be encountered by death and not to be changed by it.
Born Toward Dying
— Richard John Neuhaus

Life, death and everything in between is paradoxical; it's always a two-sided coin. We are immutably separate as humans and yet, at the same time, universally connected. No one can do your dying for you but you, yet dying is a reality that every single person shares. Emotional and spiritual suffering is painful to watch and it often disguises the important work the dying must do in transforming their suffering into meaning. We can most help the dying by compassionately allowing them this kind of struggle.

For helpers who have been groomed in traditional healthcare, companioning philosophy is a difficult transition. If we have been trained and rewarded for directing and controlling with a specific outcome in mind, we will be uncomfortable giving authority back to the dying-back to whom the experience belongs.

In a culture where mercy and nonjudgmental compassion are in short supply, the dying population we support are usually more interested in our acceptance than our advice. Though they've been conditioned to expect it, there is nothing they need to do to meet anyone's approval. They've had a lifetime of that already.

The dying have taught me they usually prefer their own wisdom over yours and mine. They will filter what we have to offer and reconfigure it into something useful to them regardless of what we intend. We must not take it personally nor be offended. It's not our show, after all.

Sometimes the dying and their families are able to reconcile personal, spiritual and family issues...sometimes not. Sometimes companions make an observable difference in their lives, sometimes not. It sometimes happens that people dying become inspired to heal old emotional wounds but may not have the physical energy or time left to grieve or mourn them. Those people will take with them to death their unreconciled matters to work on elsewhere. Forrest was right: "I guess sometimes there just aren't enough rocks."

And children are endowed with the remarkable ability to find their way, too, if they have access to stable, loving adults who will be honest, open and patient.

Finally, companioning the dying never has to be an emergency, even if others insist their emergency be yours as well. Of course, there are matters of extreme importance and every kind of anxious personality to match, but as companions, we can only do what we can only do. However distressful or dramatic a scene may look and feel, it is always in a state of adequacy if we view it with mercy rather than judgment. When we are able to make peace with our own limitations, that which we can do will always be enough.

Encouragement

My guess is that if you're reading this book, you might be someone who already knows how to work too much. So, let me be a friend who strongly supports your companioning work but equally encourages you to cultivate your life outside of companioning. Please, please develop or remain dedicated to hobbies, creative interests, travel, play or anything that doesn't look like the companioning work you do from 8 to 5. I don't know about you, but the kind of people who just make me want to drive my truck off a cliff are helping professionals who can't give it a rest.

During my workday, I try to build in simple ways to "smell the roses." My version may include listening to music in my truck between appointments or at my desk. Around my community, I've memorized the location of some of the most serene and beautiful parks, gardens and desert views. If I can, I take the scenic route to a home visit. When I know I'm going to finish my day near one of my favorite scenic areas, after my last appointment I'll park my truck, drop the tailgate and with a cup of coffee, I'll serenade a spectacular sunset on my guitar. As companions, each of us needs to do our own version of these things as a matter of inspiration and survival.

We who companion the dying cannot avoid being deeply touched by the nature of work we do. It is also common knowledge that as helpers, we are not known for our ability to practice what we often encourage others to do, such as regularly giving expression to feelings of sadness and loss. When we don't, there is a cumulative effect that is never healthy. If we are to thrive and find joy in companioning, we have to learn to become what Harvard researcher William Worden called "active grievers." Companions must learn to regularly express outwardly what we feel inwardly. That is, we need to normalize our own need to mourn on a regular basis. I'm convinced there will never be enough hours in the day to adequately debrief everything we are touched by. Yet we have to squeeze in processing time here and there with good listeners and reality-checkers.

I can usually recognize when my feelings of grief are building. I find my tears are unusually close to the surface and I feel less patient with the challenges of those I support. My ability to listen is greatly impaired and my thoughts increasingly wander off to turquoise waters and white sandy beaches. And I really know I need some time off when my inner responses begin sounding critical or judgmental.

Gratitude

Companioning the dying has gifted me with a heightened appreciation for every moment of life. Because I companion people every day who are saying goodbye to this world and those they love, I take much less for granted. What a precious thing to be able to hold my wife and children today and tell them, "I was just thinking about you and wanted to say I love you." I'm enriched with growing gratitude for the privilege of bearing witness to the intimate experiences of the dying and those who love them. What great teachers.

Having shared some part of the dying experience with many hundreds of people people by now, I've never once heard anyone say, "You know, Greg, I'm sure sorry that all those years I spent extra time with my kids or sitting on the porch swing with my beloved or watching those damn sunsets, I could have been working, watching TV or cleaning the garage!"

In the absence of loving family or friends, some who are dying yearn for comfort and validation. When they share with me a longing to know if their lives mattered (both then and now), I often ask them, "What affirming words would be the most helpful for you to hear right now?" Then as they answer, I write out their words on paper, leaving it with them to read over and over. They usually find it helpful, for they know best what they need to hear.

I decided I needed to follow my own advice, so a few years ago, during a personal crisis, I wrote out the words I most needed to hear. They continue to be grounding and still give me encouragement, often restoring some needed personal power at the right time. I keep a copy in my Daytimer and one on the wall in front of my desk at work.

I would like to invite you, dear reader, to also write for yourself the words you most need to hear. I call mine a Centering Prayer, but please honor yours with a name befitting your belief system. May you be as encouraged by yours as I have been by mine and to you all, I wish good companioning.

My Centering Prayer

Father, Mother, Creator...Remind me how deeply blessed I am to have my precious family and friends. Were I to lose everything but them, I would only be reduced to the status of richest man in the world. My good fortune would still far exceed that of so many others.

Help me find the right context to employ my gifts; Companion, father, husband, friend, musician, artist and citizen of the world. When a thousand trivialities vie to displace my gratitude, may I see my children's faces and hear the laughter of my truest.

When I begin to feel less than adequate as a helper, remind me of a thousand heartfelt gratitudes given me by patients, families, coworkers and community members.

Let me see past harsh words of others into their woundedness. Remind me to speak to their hurt and mentor their healing. And may I never miss a chance to laugh at myself.

Recall to me the soulful and poignant moments shared with the dying and bereaved that have left me forever changed in ways I cannot measure. Their lanterns have so often illuminated my own pathway.

Let me close my eyes at any moment and scan the magnificent earthly pleasures at my disposal. May I revel in the simple joys I so love.

Father, Mother, Creator... give me clearer vision into my own Heart and into the Great Heart shared by all beings. Help me live in peace with paradox knowing that I am at the same time part of a great wound and part of a great healing. May I practice mercy toward all people and all events... especially toward myself. Give me courage to trust my own belief that everything belongs. For it is with this that I agonize the most.

G.Y.